The Myth of the Out of Character Crime

The Myth of the
Out of Character Crime

༃

Stanton E. Samenow

PRAEGER

Westport, Connecticut
London

Library of Congress Cataloging-in-Publication Data

Samenow, Stanton E., 1941-
The myth of the out of character crime / Stanton E. Samenow.
   p. cm.
  Includes bibliographical references and index.
  ISBN 978–0–275–99194–4 (alk. paper)
  1. Criminal psychology. 2. Criminal behavior. 3. Criminal liability. I. Title.
HV6080.S224 2007
364.3—dc22   2007027850

British Library Cataloguing in Publication Data is available.

Library of Congress Catalog Card Number: 2007027850
ISBN-13: 978–0–275–99194–4

First published in 2007

Praeger Publishers, 88 Post Road West, Westport, CT 06881
An imprint of Greenwood Publishing Group, Inc.
www.praeger.com

Printed in the United States of America

The paper used in this book complies with the
Permanent Paper Standard issued by the National
Information Standards Organization (Z39.48-1984).

10 9 8 7 6 5 4 3 2 1

Table of Contents

Acknowledgments

I thank the following for reading drafts of this manuscript and offering excellent suggestions: MeLena Hessel, Ira Kirschbaum, Roger Lauer, and Richard Stromberg.

CHAPTER 1

The "Out of Character" Crime

*T*he theme of this book is that *people always respond in character*, that it is impossible for a person to do otherwise. You cannot be other than what you are! The "out of character" crime can be understood only by figuring out what the character of the alleged perpetrator truly is. "Character" as used here is synonymous with the patterns of thinking and behavior that a person demonstrates throughout life. If you do something out of character, you are not being you. That is impossible!

From time to time, accounts burst into the news of regular, everyday people who unexpectedly do hideous things. They commit crimes that shock their communities and stun even individuals who know them extremely well. Parents, spouses, relatives, friends, neighbors, work colleagues, and others who have close, even intimate, relationships with these people are at a loss to understand what has happened. When they learn of the crime while watching the evening news or reading the morning paper, their first thought is that the person they know could not possibly be the perpetrator because it is totally "out of character."

Think about it. Having known your friend for years, you consider him a person of impeccable integrity. You are incredulous when you read that he has embezzled thousands of dollars from his employer and invested it in a get-rich-quick scheme. You admire a neighbor who, upon emigrating to this country from his war-shattered homeland, overcame many adversities while educating himself and obtaining a position as a respected scientist. Suddenly, you learn that this accomplished, quiet, self-effacing individual has been charged with abducting a man at gunpoint. Imagine being in love with a fellow who seems almost perfect. Good-looking, charming, well educated, and with a promising professional future, he is focused on establishing himself in a medical practice. Your dreams are shattered when you learn he has been taken into custody for stalking and terrifying a young woman. Or consider the kid you know down the street. He has wonderful parents who have been good neighbors. You've not heard one bad thing about the youngster. Then you find out that he has been arrested for the murder of another teenager.

In these and many other instances, the crime seemed totally out of line with the alleged perpetrator's talents, accomplishments, and reputation in the community. How can an introvert who seemed kind and generous to everyone have it within himself to murder? How is it that a woman trusted for years by her employer steals thousands of dollars from his business? And how could a gregarious, clean-cut looking professional get arrested for sexually molesting young boys?

I have been a forensic psychologist for 37 years. "Forensic" means that I am a psychologist who analyzes matters that come before courts. During a career of evaluating and treating offenders, I have come to know men, women, and children who have committed crimes that seemed completely alien to their nature. Some of these individuals have become notorious even before their identity is known because their crimes have made headlines.

During 2003, I spent 34 hours interviewing Lee Malvo, the 18-year-old Washington, D.C., sniper. When a charismatic individual like Mr. Malvo commits a horrendous crime, the human mind tries to make sense of what happened. Malvo had no prior criminal record. He showed promise of success at everything he undertook. Until he was arrested with John Muhammad for murdering people just going about their daily lives, no one would have considered Lee Malvo dangerous to anyone. In fact, at his Virginia capital murder trial, Malvo's father, teachers, relatives, and friends rallied to his defense as character witnesses.

Whether or not the cases are high-profile, my job remains the same—to be a psychological sleuth. I must make sense of behavior that no one predicted or could understand. My task is to explain the unexplainable.

There is a strong human need to understand behavior that is shocking and hard to fathom. When a seemingly out of character crime occurs,

I often receive inquiries from television and radio stations, newspapers and magazines asking me to conjecture why the person did what he or she was alleged to have done and to explain what sort of individual would do such a thing.

The individuals whom I interview are referred to me by attorneys for psychological evaluation either prior to standing trial or after they are convicted but before sentencing occurs. I have conducted evaluations at the request of both defense lawyers and prosecutors. In some instances, family members request that I evaluate the person for a particular purpose such as determining whether he is amenable to treatment and, if so, what the proper treatment would be. In plain terms, the purpose of the evaluation, no matter the referral source, is to find out who these people really are in order to help a judge, a jury, or perhaps staff in a correctional or treatment facility make more informed decisions.

These evaluations are conducted in a variety of settings. If the person is still living in the community (e.g., out on bond), I interview him in my office if the case is local. Otherwise, I go wherever he is. If he is incarcerated, I meet with him in a local adult or juvenile detention center or at a prison or psychiatric facility. After introducing myself (or being introduced), I must ascertain whether the person understands why I am interviewing him, establish what the limits are to confidentiality, and inform him how the evaluation results will be used.

The cases I discuss in this book are real, none hypothetical. With the exception of the section on Washington, D.C., sniper Lee Malvo, I am not using the actual names of defendants. Additional measures have been taken to disguise their identity.

"Out of character" means not within the character of the individual. For example, a table is not equipped to fly. It never will fly, but human beings are sometimes thought to behave in a manner alien to their own nature. It is as though sinister forces invade and take over the personality, causing the individual to do something totally unexpected. I will show that, like the table, the seemingly absent characteristics were always present in the person. But before exploring further what appears to be "out of character," we need to take a look at what we mean by "in character."

CHAPTER 2

Thinking Errors as a Key to Character

We develop characteristic ways of thinking, feeling, and behaving that form the core of who we are. These patterns are consistent over time. They play a critical role in how we cope with events in daily life. In combination with one another, they make us unique. They are enduring and form the bedrock of our personality.

The words "character" and "personality" are used interchangeably, both in common speech and in professional discourse by psychologists. The dictionary definitions are extremely close to each other. *Character*, according to *The Random House Dictionary of the English Language*, is defined as "the aggregate of features and traits that form the apparent individual nature of some person or thing."[1] *Personality* is defined as "the sum total of the physical, mental, emotional, and social characteristics of an individual."[2] If we remark that a person behaved "in character," it means that the conduct was consistent with his personality as we know it. "Out of character" means not in keeping with that personality.

It takes a very long time to know the many dimensions of an individual's personality well enough to assess accurately what is "in character." What a person presents publicly often differs radically from what he is like privately. The brilliant and compassionate physician whom we have consulted for years might not be so admirable if we lived with him. The outgoing, affable neighbor with whom we enjoy chatting may be a coarse, insensitive tyrant to the family who knows him intimately.

We would be shocked to see a police car pull up to the home of a person we like and admire and then see that person escorted out the door in handcuffs.

In the physical world, causality usually is not difficult to determine. Newton's third law of motion states, "For every action, there is an equal and opposite reaction." Water freezes at a temperature of 32 degrees Fahrenheit. A punctured balloon loses air. In the world of human behavior, identifying causes is usually not so straightforward. The nature versus nurture controversy and all that it entails endures. Analysts of human behavior take into account biological (including genetic) factors, socio-economic contributors, and childhood experience. Even the most avid determinists acknowledge that personal choice plays a critical role in our behavior.

Behavior is the direct result of the way a person thinks. This is a very old concept articulated in the proverb, "As a man thinketh, so is he." As a psychologist working in the area of criminal behavior, I have found that thinking errors are causal in every case of criminal conduct. Throughout this book, I will focus on patterns of thinking that provide clues to the personality of the individual.

From time to time, all of us make what I call "thinking errors." (This term has been adopted over the years by corrections and mental health professionals who work with offenders in community and institutional programs designed to help them change.) When present to an extreme, in combination with one another, the thinking errors give rise to irresponsible or illegal conduct. For example, a highly responsible individual may blurt out something without considering the repercussions and then, to his consternation, discover he has hurt someone's feelings. Whereas even the most responsible person may make occasional errors of thinking, they are not part of a criminal pattern. They reflect gaps in foresight, sensitivity, and judgment. For a self-absorbed person who sees himself as the center of the universe, disregard for the impact of his behavior on other people is a *pattern*, and thus endemic to his way of life.

What do I mean by an *error* in thinking? From the standpoint of the individual doing the thinking, he is not making an error. He's just going about living his life. His thoughts are his thoughts, and they form the basis for what he says and does. The *error* is a flaw in the thought process that usually results in behavior that injures or, at the very least, inconveniences others. The more extensive the pattern of an error of thinking, the greater the injury.

I snap at an airport gate agent for not announcing why my flight's departure is delayed. At least two errors in thinking underlie my conduct. One is that I am making an assumption that she knows more than she is disclosing. A second is that, through a display of temper, I will gain more control and therefore be more likely to obtain the information. There are negative consequences to these errors in thinking, potentially both to her and to me. By hassling her, I make her life more difficult. She has only whatever information is made available to her. My anger is unlikely to elicit more information. In fact, the gate agent may try to avoid dealing with me at all. So what I have done is self-defeating. Had my inquiry been polite, I still may have learned nothing new about the status of the flight. However, I would not have added a dose of unpleasantness to her day.

Richard is on the phone with Tanya, his ex-wife. He is screaming because she is late returning the children to him. Tanya responds by cursing a blue streak. Their two young children are cowering in the hallway while overhearing their mother's part of the conversation. She slams down the phone and yells at them to hurry and get into the car, meanwhile denouncing their dad as a first-class jerk. Once the children are in, she speeds off. They arrive at Richard's and are greeted by his furiously threatening Tanya that he will sue her for contempt of the court order that establishes specific visitation hours. The errors in thinking are as follows:

- Richard is assuming that his ex-wife is being intentionally late just to provoke him;
- Richard is overreacting to the lateness by interpreting it personally as a deliberate putdown;
- Both Richard and Tanya are using anger to control the other;
- Both parents seem oblivious to the impact of their behavior on their children who are the innocent victims.

If Tanya had remained calm instead of throwing a tantrum, she would not have inflamed Richard further. Tanya could have tried to explain why she was running late and apologized. Whether Richard accepted what she said was beyond her control. At least, while the children were with Tanya, they could have been spared a great deal of the unpleasantness, which had nothing to do with them. The point is that errors in thinking often result in injury to others!

People who are extremely responsible make errors in thinking. Individuals other than adjudicated offenders lie. A child knocks over a glass of milk and claims that the cat did it. An employee calls in sick, whereas he really wants a day off to play golf. You tell a person that his tie is attractive, whereas you wouldn't wear it even if it were given to you.

There is a major difference, quantitatively and qualitatively, between the person who lies once in a while and the person who lies as a way of life. If you have ever lived or worked with a chronic liar, you know how unsettling it is. The person covers up wrongdoing, or he concocts a story after you discover something he did and confront him. Just as distressing is that he lies for no apparent reason. Lies seem to roll off his tongue as habitually as he breathes. Occasionally, he tells the truth about something important. More likely, he relates part of the truth while giving the impression that he is being completely honest. Having established a modicum of trust frees him to lie even more later. Lies that seem to make no sense actually do have a purpose once you understand the mentality of the chronic liar. From his vantage point, lying is exciting. By lying, he preserves a view of himself as an individual who can easily outsmart others. Pulling the wool over people's eyes is exciting and enhances his sense of power. The chronic liar has victims, especially people with whom he lives and works.

While interviewing an offender, a trained investigator can identify errors in thinking and not waste time on a psychological fishing expedition, which can entail trying to elicit information that will neatly accommodate a theory he already has in mind.

Another example of a thinking error is a person's tendency to procrastinate. From time to time, we all postpone attending to an unpleasant chore or obligation. The consequences of such a delay may be minor. If we put off cutting the grass, it grows higher and requires more time and effort once we finally attend to it. If we delay a mortgage or rent payment, we may be assessed a hefty late fee. Some people rarely procrastinate. They appear driven, even compulsive, about being prompt. An unpaid bill or an unfulfilled obligation preys upon their minds until they take care of it. At the other extreme are people who constantly delay, even to the point of ignoring an obligation and experience smug satisfaction, even excitement, because they got away with it. They think that they are not obliged to do anything unless it suits their mood or objective at the time. Their habitual thinking seems to be, "If I feel like it, fine; if not, forget it." There are consequences, some serious, to chronic procrastination, because other people are adversely affected. The person who thinks that household chores are unimportant or perhaps beneath him antagonizes people he lives with. When he fails to pay bills, he incurs penalties, and creditors pursue him. When he is late completing work assignments, co-workers may be inconvenienced. The procrastinator feels under siege when others take him to task. Thinking he is being singled out and mistreated, he tries to deflect the focus from his own irresponsibility by finding fault with others who are fed up with him. Refusing to face up to problems he created, he further incurs the distrust and wrath of others. In a confrontation over his procrastination, he may blow up at the person holding him accountable, then, thinking he'll teach that individual a lesson, assault him or destroy his property.

Procrastination may appear of minor interest or even irrelevant to an investigator such as myself. Considered by itself, it may not be especially important. However, combined with other thinking patterns, it may have played a contributory role to the perpetrator's committing a crime. Take the following situation. Sam pays Barbara $1,000 a month for child support. He is three months in arrears. He thinks it won't matter now because Barbara has been pretty low key when he has been behind in the past. However, Barbara currently is running low on funds and needs the money. Their relationship, already strained, deteriorates further. When she threatens him with a law suit, he is consumed by thoughts of retaliating. He explodes, calls her names and threatens her with bodily harm. After Barbara has court papers served on Sam, she finds the tires of her car slashed. Why did Sam procrastinate? It wasn't because he was poor. Rather, he had other priorities—spending money on himself for a big screen television, souping up his car, and betting on sports events.

Another thinking error is making an instant decision that turns out to be costly. In a store, you spot merchandise that you want then and there. You immediately purchase it only to find the next week a less expensive product that is of better quality. It's too late! You overpaid and are stuck with the inferior item. Many of us have been in a similar position.

Stung once, we are more careful the next time. Consider the shopper who habitually thinks "I've got to have it now" and makes snap decisions. The mere process of acquiring things gives her a rush. She buys items for which she has no possible use. With no end to her reckless expenditures, she racks up huge bills while hiding purchases from her husband. When the bills arrive, her spouse is taken aback and furious, but she doesn't curtail her spending. The money he works so hard for is disappearing, and they are now in debt. His trust in her is shattered.

Profligate spending resulting in substantial debt is irresponsible. It is a consequence of thinking errors that include the following:

- Thinking "I want it; I must have it now";
- Failure to ascertain facts, weigh alternatives (e.g., comparison shop), and make a more responsible decision;
- Failure to establish priorities and plan ahead while delaying gratification;
- Failure to consider potential consequences to others.

The issue for the forensic psychologist is to note the pattern and determine how it plays out in the life of the defendant being evaluated. Is profligate spending simply a bad habit, or is it the tip of an iceberg of other reckless behavior? The key concept is *pattern*. Every young child who steals a candy bar does not become a one-man walking crime wave.

My objective initially is to get to know the person, specifically how he thinks. For hours, I may not discuss the crime at issue. Instead, I seek to obtain a picture of how the offender has functioned in various areas of life. Understandably, he is likely to be defensive about the act for which he is in legal jeopardy. He is inclined to be far more candid when asked to discuss aspects of life that he thinks are not related to the crime.

At this point, you might wonder how the word "crime" is being used. A particular act might be considered a crime in one state but not another. Laws change, redefining what is considered "criminal." Homosexual behavior even in private among consenting adults was deemed a crime in many states. Once the laws changed, such conduct was not illegal.

In this book, I cite cases from my practice in which individuals are charged with breaking the law. However, my concept of criminality deals not only with specific laws at a particular place and time, but extends to how people live their lives. Some individuals would be criminals no matter how the laws read or where they live. One man commented, "If rape were legalized today, I wouldn't rape. I would do something else." In his thinking, to be a person who matters is to do what is forbidden, whatever that might be. In a neverending quest to establish himself, he invariably victimizes others, using deception, intimidation, or brute force.

Criminal behavior, as I conceive of it, refers to conduct that injures people, whether physically, emotionally, or financially. A person might behave "criminally" without breaking laws. Unfortunately, most of us have encountered at least one person who incessantly lies to get what he wants, controls others with his temper, and selfishly pursues his objectives without thinking about whom he hurts. An example would be a man who rules his family with an iron fist and uses his temper as a means of control. Even if he has not broken the law, such a tyrant has his victims every day. His wife and children walk on eggshells, constantly fearful he will explode if they upset him. It is likely that, eventually, he will commit a crime by erupting in anger and destroying property or assaulting a family member.

I can spot errors in thinking as the offender discusses almost any aspect of life. For example, a young man charged with first degree murder bragged about how he conned therapist after therapist to whom his desperate parents dragged him. He gloated as he described the well-intentioned men and women who wanted to help him as though they were buffoons. As he boasted to me of his shenanigans in therapy, he was revealing aspects of his character. Three thinking errors contributed to his behavior. First, he failed to think about the impact of his lying, stealing, and drug use on others, especially his parents, who cared most about him. Second, instead of utilizing a therapist to help, he thought of him as a person to overcome. Believing he had successfully pulled the wool over a therapist's eyes boosted his self-image. Third, he did not think about potential adverse consequences to himself of being combative with his parents and resistant to therapists. As you will see, obtaining such information is essential to developing an understanding of what is "in character."

Tony savagely attacked and killed a relative. He told me how depressed he had been long before he committed the crime. He said that he had become despondent because he was out of money, worked at a boring job for an irascible boss, and lived with his grandfather, who was unreasonably hard on him. Tony saw little hope of improving his situation. A therapist was treating him for depression with therapy and medication. As I questioned him about his circumstances, I learned a great deal about how Tony thought. This man had a menial and boring job because he refused to stick with any job long enough to acquire skills. If a task was boring or difficult, he wanted little or no part of it. Tony was perpetually low on funds because he sometimes refused to work at all and, when he did work, showed up erratically. Tony's heartless boss turned out to be a man who put up with his tardiness and arriving at the job site hung over. In his characteristic black and white thinking, Tony thought any individual who criticized him was totally against him. Rather than fulfill the requirements of others, he insisted that they fulfill his requirements. Tony caused his own "depression" by his irresponsibility. No antidepressant could cure that! Although this information was not directly related to the crime, it provided insight into Tony's personality by illuminating the way he thought. This man's close-to-the-surface anger at anyone who thwarted him, even in very minor ways, played a role in the homicide.

Knowledge of how a person thinks unlocks the key to his character. While discussing particular cases, I shall indicate what errors in thinking came to light and then show how they provided clues to understanding the crime. Clearly, my psychological studies are conducted *after* the crime has been committed and a person has been arrested.

I believe that, upon concluding this book, the reader will understand that errors in thinking did not originate in adulthood. Although we may not be able to predict with certainty who will commit a crime in the future, being able to identify errors of thinking in children could lead to interventions (without pejorative labeling) that will prevent a tremendous amount of destruction in the future.

In this book, I focus on people who have been criminally charged by federal or local law enforcement authorities. These men and women have committed a wide variety of property, assaultive, sexual, and drug- and alcohol-related offenses. In a few cases, a defendant was referred for evaluation of his sanity at the time he committed the crime.

NOTES

1. Stein, Jess and Laurence Urdang (Eds.) *The Random House Dictionary of the English Language*. New York: Random House, 1987, p. 346.

2. Stein, Jess and Laurence Urdang (Eds.) *The Random House Dictionary of the English Language*. NY: Random House, 1987, p. 1445.

CHAPTER 3

Realities about the "Out of Character" Crime

A frequent explanation for a person behaving out of character is that he "snapped" because of the stress of an unanticipated and traumatic situation, such as being fired from a job, suffering a devastating financial reversal, or being uprooted by a natural disaster. Or a person behaved out of character when his psychological defenses broke down after weeks, months, or years of enduring a chronically stressful situation.

Unanticipated and severely stressful events occur in nearly everyone's life. We all suffer loss, disappointment, one hardship or another. Human beings adopt an attitude toward adversity that is consistent with their character. The critical issue is not what happens to a person, but how he chooses to cope with whatever life doles out. Consider the impact of a sudden traumatic experience. Without advance notice, an employee receives a "pink slip" notifying him he no longer has a job because new management is taking over. Suddenly, he is unable to support his family. There are many possible reactions to such a devastating, unexpected event. A person may become so depressed and psychologically immobilized that he remains at home doing nothing to improve his situation. Another fantasizes "getting even" but takes no action. A third person returns to the job site and angrily confronts his former supervisor at gunpoint. And a fourth individual immediately starts searching out leads for a new job. The individual responds in a manner consistent with how he has reacted to other major stresses. A person who has dealt with past set-backs by taking constructive measures to improve his situation will not endanger others or himself by engaging in a violent confrontation.

When Hurricane Katrina struck the Gulf Coast in 2005, some residents fled their homes as soon as they heard the warning that a major hurricane might strike. Some remained although they had the resources to leave. Others took advantage of the chaos that descended in the storm's aftermath. News accounts told of looters and other predators exploiting the situation for personal gain. The reactions of people afflicted by such tragedies are in keeping with their personality. A responsible person will not maraud through abandoned streets stealing whatever he can grab.

Consider a situation in which a person endures prolonged stress that is physically and emotionally debilitating. A woman discovers that her husband is not the sweet, devoted person she thought he was when they first married. He belittles her, isolates her from friends and family, berates her when she fails to do what he wants, and sexually and physically mistreats her. One response is resignation. The abused spouse stays in the situation, convinced that she deserves the harsh treatment and believing she'd be no better off if she tried to leave. A submissive woman with little self-confidence may think that if she changes, her husband will treat her better. Then there is the woman who rids herself of her tormentor by killing him, expecting that a judge will understand and excuse her behavior. Still another response is for the woman to devise a plan to leave, implement that plan, then take measures to protect herself in case she is pursued.

In facing any adversity, a range of responses is possible. A person behaves in line with his or her overall personality makeup.

You might inquire, "Doesn't everyone have a breaking point?" Consider a person experiencing a series of setbacks, disappointments, or just plain bad luck. Each time he gets knocked down, he staggers to his feet and keeps going. Finally, he can't take anymore, and the one thing that is too much to endure pushes him over the edge. Isn't that precisely when a person does something out of character?

People differ in attitude toward adversity. For many, the saying is true that when the going gets tough, the tough get going. There are men and women who every day of their lives battle continuous, debilitating health problems. Some parents experience agonizing stress for years as they struggle to help their child cope with severe developmental and learning disabilities. There are entrepreneurs who have struggled to establish a business only to see their venture eventually collapse because of economic factors beyond their control. There are innumerable examples of human beings who grapple daily with all sorts of problems that plague them unrelentingly. If we know these people personally, we marvel at how they manage, especially when each day seems to offer little hope of relief. Many of these individuals maintain a cheerful demeanor, seldom complain, and put one foot in front of the other to deal with their lot. What might be the "one thing too much" for one person is to another just one more adversity to cope with.

Of course, even those who appear the most stalwart waver, despair, and become discouraged and resentful. Nonetheless, their overall attitude is to respond to adversity as a challenge and renew their determination to cope. They show an amazing degree of resilience and may inspire others.

What people perceive as constituting "adversity" may vary. At one extreme is the person with a criminal personality who sees adversity in virtually any aspect of life that does not go the way he wants. When a driver beeps the horn at him, he takes it personally and retaliates by pursuing the offending motorist. This is likely to be just one of many events occurring during a single day when others do not fulfill his unrealistic expectations or yield to his demands. Such a person creates his own adversity by responding angrily, then blaming others for what happens.

During an evaluation, Bob told me that he got so "stressed out" at his job that he couldn't take anymore and finally quit. When I asked him about the source of the stress, he told me that he'd frequently come to work hung over. When his supervisor saw that he was impaired on the job, he reprimanded Bob and sent him home without pay. As this happened frequently, the supervisor was not eager for Bob to remain part of his work crew. Bob contended that the stress for him was being a slave to a task master who never was satisfied. By arriving at work with a bad attitude and sometimes in no physical condition to work, Bob caused the very situation that he resented. The boss was not irascible with other employees who were doing what they were supposed to.

It doesn't take much for an individual with Bob's personality to become angry. The one thing too much that sets him off may seem quite

trivial—his wife speaking sharply to him, a customer at work complaining, or encountering a rude store clerk. Quick to take offense, his
response is out of proportion to the significance of the incident. When
contending with problems not of his own making, a responsible person
endeavors to retain his composure and cope with the situation rather than
make it worse. Instead of reacting as though his entire self-image is on
the line, he looks for solutions. He reacts to his irritated wife with humor.
He tries to placate a disgruntled customer rather than win an argument.
Realizing that a store clerk may be having a bad day, he doesn't take her
rudeness personally

Drugs can affect a person's behavior, but do they cause him to react out
of character? I recall one fellow saying, "I didn't kill him; the drugs did
it." He declared that if it weren't for drugs, the crime would never have
occurred. This is an after the fact rationalization. Who chose to embark
on the way of life that he had been living for years, against the advice
and pleading of his family and others? Who made the decision to use
drugs, then risk his life by roaming dangerous city streets to obtain
drugs? The homicidal thinking and behavior were not *caused* by
the drugs. The thinking was already present! Using a mind-altering
substance eliminated psychological barriers to its expression.

Drugs knock out the fear of consequences and restraints of conscience.
What the person thought about but was inhibited from doing, he now
does. As a person becomes intoxicated by drug use, he becomes emboldened, and the genie leaves the bottle. Put another way, 10 drunk men
would not behave similarly. A man unaccustomed to heavy drinking
might fall asleep. Another might start telling off-color jokes. Other reactions might include becoming loud and boisterous, growing belligerent,
provoking a physical confrontation, and jumping into a car and driving
off at a high speed. Anything is possible, including abducting a woman
and raping her, but the critical determining factor is the personality of
the user before he consumed the alcohol.

The crime does not reside within the bottle, the powder, the syringe, or
the pill. The substance brings out whatever tendencies already reside
within the user. Others may never have seen the behavior or had any
forewarning. There still is precedent for the behavior. A man who kills
has most likely been violent before or, innumerable times, has fantasized
assaulting others.

Finally, one might contend that if a person who never has been in a fight attacks someone while defending himself, he nonetheless is behaving out of character. At first blush, this might appear to be the case because the individual is reacting in a manner that is contrary to his lifelong avoidance of violence. But we would have to know more details. Did he try to escape? Did he try to negotiate, bargain, or in some way dissuade his assailant? Even if he could do nothing other than fight for his life, he would find the experience terrifying, not exciting. There would be gratitude, not bragging, about what it took to survive. The aftermath might be suffering panic attacks, nightmares, and flashbacks, not a boost to his ego. This is quite different from a person who provokes and enjoys fighting, like the young man who told me that he loves hearing the crack of bones and seeing the flow of blood when he lashes out at anyone who dares to "disrespect" him.

We think that we know what is "in character" for family members, neighbors, co-workers and others with whom we have close contact. To believe that it was an acutely stressful situation, chronic stress, the "one thing too much," or drug use that caused a person to behave out of character indicates merely that we did not know as much as we thought we did about that individual. In conducting a psychological evaluation, it is my job to find a context for the crime, to figure out the true character of the perpetrator.

Chapter 4

Secret Controllers

*P*eople who commit serious crimes are determined to control others. Their self-esteem depends upon it! Some are obvious about their quest for control because they bully and threaten. Others smoothly insinuate themselves into the lives of their eventual prey, maneuvering so deftly that their motives are not evident.

Exercising control over people is neither good nor bad. The question is how one pursues and exercises it. Some roles in life, by their very nature, require a person to have authority over others. A parent is expected to control his child and teach him limits. A teacher controls students in her class by requiring them to adhere to academic, social, and behavioral standards. A police officer, entrusted to protect the community, exercises control even by force if necessary while making an arrest.

Some people have substantial control over others because they have earned a position through hard work and achievement. An employee who works hard and rises through the ranks to become a corporate executive gains considerable authority over the company's employees. The mayor of a city is elected by citizens who entrust him with far-reaching power.

Responsible individuals do not abuse their authority. They are more focused on serving others than being self-serving. Others, dissatisfied with what they have attained by legitimate means, misuse authority entrusted to them and exploit their position for their own self-aggrandizement.

Exercising control over others as a legitimate function of one's position is one thing. Control for the sake of control is an error in thinking in which the person regards interpersonal relationships as arenas for conquests, conquests that are vital to propping up his self-image but which also lead to emotional, financial, or physical casualties.

The mother who micromanages her teenage daughter's life in order to fulfill her own needs is bound to create unnecessary conflict and cause psychological damage. The policeman who misuses his authority may get into trouble with his supervisor as well as enrage the public. Occasionally, we read about law enforcement officers who have been overzealous in their use of force or who have in other ways betrayed their position of public trust. The corporate executive who creates a climate where subordinates constantly fear displeasing him is misusing his power.

In their unending quest to control others, such individuals fortify an insatiable psychological need. Their legitimately attained position is utilized as a vehicle to build up an already inflated ego. They treat others like pawns on their own personal chessboard. Many of these individuals are extremely intelligent, talented, and successful. While appearing sensitive to others, they conceal their true intentions. What matters most is prevailing in any situation, and they will resort to any means to gain what they want. Because they are admired, their faults are not recognized or are overlooked. People put up with their exploitive and abusive behavior. This in turn reinforces their mounting sense of invincibility.

Jill, a middle-aged lady, came to me desperate for help. She had devoted a decade to a relationship with Ted, a man whom she eventually came to fear. Ted, a respected professional, had been financially generous to her and her children. Insecure because of earlier unsuccessful relationships with men, Jill was gratified that this wonderful man had remained committed to her for so long. Ted had his dark moods and could be quite unpleasant when his judgment was questioned, but Jill forgave him repeatedly and even thought that perhaps she caused most of the problems in their relationship. Although he never hit her, Ted's cutting sarcasm and belittling remarks were so demoralizing that Jill started to think she could do nothing right. She was jolted into realizing that Ted had serious problems having nothing to do with her when she mistakenly opened mail addressed to him and learned that he had been compelled to surrender his professional license. Ted had no idea that Jill had seen legal documents setting forth complaints that he had exploited and sadistically injured his clients. Jill began to put a number of things together and then felt all the worse because she had been gullible enough to get conned. She was in a terrible predicament because she had quit her job and become financially dependent on Ted. Feeling imprisoned in the relationship, she did not know how to break free.

Controllers like Ted conceal the sinister motives that drive them. Like Jill, others are taken in and fail to condemn misconduct that they would not tolerate in others. Admirers of such people do not perceive them as malevolent and often believe they can do no wrong. People like Ted count on this!

I call these individuals "secret controllers" because they are not perceived as controlling. They are remarkably successful at obtaining what they want, and rarely do others challenge them. These individuals may not be seen for who they really are until they have done irreparable harm. They may gain political power. Jim Jones, the notorious cult leader, established the community of Jonestown in Guayana, South America, where, in 1978, he convinced some 900 believers to commit suicide by drinking cyanide-laced punch.

When the secret controller is confronted by a major threat to his ego, his response may be cataclysmic, appearing completely out of character. Such was the case with Steven, a talented young scientist with no criminal record who was arrested for abducting a man, handcuffing him, and threatening to blow off his head with a pistol. If ever there seemed to be an out of character crime, this was it. The probation officer charged with preparing the pre-sentence report was so baffled by Steven's conduct that she asked the court to order a psychological evaluation. I became involved after a judge ordered that this young man be examined "to determine the nature and extent of any pre-existing or existing mental and/or emotional problem."

One might expect a defendant facing a substantial prison sentence to be so apprehensive that, for a court-ordered evaluation, he would set his best foot forward or, at the very least, appear compliant, whatever his misgivings might be. My introduction to this man was to encounter a barrage of complaints and objections. Steven groused about the early morning hour of the meeting. He criticized the wording of my questions.

He maintained that the entire process was unnecessary because he already had met several times with a counselor who could write a report.

The interview proceeded like a chess game. Anything I said, Steven countered. After 40 minutes of skirmishing, Steven remained unrelenting in his tactical maneuvers by which he intended to control all aspects of our meeting. Realizing we had reached an impasse, I picked up the phone and called the probation officer, then asked Steven to speak with her. She informed him that a letter from his counselor would not quality as a psychological evaluation. Despite her urging him to cooperate with me, Steven continued to object to the process and questioned how I would reach conclusions. I did my best to answer his questions, but as soon as I replied to one, more were forthcoming.

You might see nothing unusual about this. In fact, you might think it quite sensible for a highly intelligent person to question a process upon which his future depends. But Steven was doing more than this. He appeared to be vying for total control.

Steven had been taking charge of situations since he was 10 years old. His parents left Cambodia to establish a home for the family in the United States, leaving him and his siblings in the care of elderly grandparents. Steven took it upon himself to keep his brothers and sister in line. A sister told me that Steven was "like a brother and a father." Once the entire family had settled in the United States, Steven's role was well-established. His sister commented that when she had a problem, she never sought her father's advice but, instead, confided in Steven. She described her brother with near reverence, commenting on how he helped the family and praising him for his generosity, studiousness, and many accomplishments.

Steven was successful at every undertaking. He taught himself English and studied in the library until late at night. His persistence paid off. He ranked first in his high school graduating class and was elected class president. He readily gained admission to a prestigious college, which granted him a four year scholarship. Achieving collegiate academic honors, he was courted by graduate schools that offered him funding for his studies and stipends for living expenses.

Steven had demonstrated that he was a determined individual who was willing to work hard and do whatever was necessary to achieve his goals. He permitted nothing to thwart him. Failure was not part of

Steven's experience. He was a leader in every setting: at home, at school, and at church, where he led a Bible study group. So accustomed was he to being in control of people that he eventually concluded, "If everything goes your way, you don't need God."

Until his first romantic involvement, Steven seemed able to overcome any adversity. He told me, "Until I met Helen, everything went smoothly." He became enamored of this young woman while working at a summer job. Within a year, he concluded that she was the person whom he'd marry. When I asked if Helen was equally in love with him, Steven replied, "I fell in love quicker." Helen had reservations.

Admiring her artistic ability, Steven persuaded Helen to switch her major to fine arts. This required an additional year of course work. Helen told Steven they should see each other less often so that she could apply herself more to academics. Steven reacted by doing what he always did when he encountered an obstacle—redoubling his efforts. Finished with graduate school and holding a full time job, Steven thought nothing of driving several hundred miles to visit his girlfriend. Helen recalled, "He'd ask to come up. I'd say 'no'. He'd just come. He'd ignore my request and do what *he* wanted." When she stood firm about his not visiting, Steven besieged her with phone calls. Helen found it impossible to hold fast in setting limits.

Steven intruded on other aspects of Helen's life. Some nights, she did not arrive home until late from the library or art studio. Steven scolded her like a child for risking her safety. He insisted that if she was going to be out late, she had to call him. Helen responded by doing what was easiest, submitting to whatever Steven demanded. However, she remained adamant about refusing to have sexual intercourse. Steven did not take well to this!

It was Steven's belief that Helen had cooled on their relationship for a reason that remained unstated but had nothing to do with her program of studies. Helen confided in Steven something that she had disclosed to no one else. At age five, and again as a teenager, her uncle had molested her. Steven pressed for details and kept churning the whole thing over in his mind. This was a problem that he was certain Helen needed help with even though she had not asked for assistance. And so he hounded her, grilling her about the most minute details of what transpired. Helen was dismayed and offended by Steven's constant invasion of her privacy. She endured his interrogations, convinced that he was doing it out of love.

In characteristic fashion, Steven decided to take charge: "I wouldn't put it aside. It was something I had to take care of." Steven told me that it was obligation, comparable to watching out for his siblings when their parents left them as youngsters in Cambodia with their grandparents. As Helen became less available, Steven became more determined to rectify the injustice perpetrated years ago against Helen by her uncle. Steven was certain that once he psychologically and sexually liberated Helen, she would be his forever.

Over many months, Steven pondered how to achieve his objective. He resolved to track down the uncle and have him apologize directly to Helen. He told me that eliciting the truth and an apology could occur only if the uncle were under duress. "That's why I picked the violent way," Steven explained. Eleven months before he took action, he concluded that force would be necessary. According to police reports, Steven came into possession of a gun and ammunition either by purchasing them directly or having someone else buy them. Investigators also learned that Steven completed a course in which he learned how to use firearms.

What his true intentions were, only Steven knew. In a statement to law enforcement officers, Helen's uncle related his terrifying ordeal. Steven tracked him down, at gun point forced him out of the car, applied hand-cuffs, and warned him not to do anything stupid. Steven terrorized the uncle by rubbing the gun against his head, informing him that he had killed before (which was not true), and warning he would not hesitate to do so again. He drove to a secluded location and began questioning the man. To the uncle's relief, police officers appeared and rescued him.

During one of our interviews, Steven cited a saying, "If you can control inside, you can control outside." Steven had a self-discipline of iron. With his stellar educational and career accomplishments, he became convinced that he could control all aspects of his life. Steven's attempt to "control outside" clearly went awry during his first serious romantic involvement.

Steven did not think he had hurt anyone. He seemed to regard himself as the victim, having been prevented from completing a benevolent mission. Rather than thinking he should seek forgiveness, he begged God to grant him "the power" to forgive Helen's uncle, whom he deemed "the worst person on earth." As for Helen, Steven declared, "I know she thinks about me. Helen will forgive, and I'll go on." He expressed his hope that the two of them would spend their future together.

I am describing Steven as a "secret controller" because most people who knew him would not have had this view. From what I could discern by talking to a sister, his siblings did not regard Steven as controlling. Quite the contrary; they looked to him for guidance. He took charge practically from the time they set foot on U.S. soil. Watching Steven's successes, his brothers and sister saw him as a role model. At school, fellow students and his teachers held Steven in the highest esteem as he mastered English, achieved honor roll grades, and was recruited by college admissions officers. He gained recognition everywhere for his unflagging effort and excellent performance. Steven did not encounter any major obstacle to his objectives until he became involved with Helen. It was impossible at first for her to believe that her boyfriend was anything but the wonderful, attentive, talented man with whom she had fallen in love. When Steven began pressuring her, Helen told herself he was acting out of concern and love. She failed to grasp that a person who truly loved her would not have badgered her, demanded to know what she was doing every moment, and psychologically browbeat her about sensitive, intimate matters. Helen would have been shocked to learn that Steven owned a gun, much less that he planned to use it to remove what he was convinced was the only barrier to their having a sexual relationship.

Because Steven immediately regarded me as a potential threat, someone whom he could not control, his own controlling personality came to the fore and became immediately evident.

As we continue to talk about people who commit crimes that appear out of character, the thinking error of aiming to control others to fortify their self-esteem will loom as a major factor.

CHAPTER 5

Sociological and Psychological Determinism: Road to a Dead End

Criminal clients come from all walks of life. They range in education from grade school dropouts to graduates of leading universities and graduate schools. Some have never held a job for longer than a few months at a time, while others are at the pinnacle of professional careers. Their backgrounds are varied—from growing up in poverty and deprivation to being raised among affluence and opportunity.

In trying to understand *why* people commit crimes, it is not just contemporary sociologists who have emphasized the role of the social environment. In the nineteenth century, the "positivist school" focused on the importance of social factors as a breeding ground for crime. This emphasis continued through the twentieth century and now into the current century. The conventional wisdom is that if a person grows up in a poor, gang-infested neighborhood where the American dream seems out of reach, turning to crime is an adaptive response (a sociological term). This thinking remains alive and well in some quarters. However, it is just plain wrong and has served as a distraction to understanding and combating crime.

Ramsey Clark, a U.S. Attorney General in the 1960s, declared that poverty is the "fountainhead" of crime.[1] We know, however, that most poor people are not criminals, and many well-to-do people are. Crime is not restricted to any economic, social, racial, or ethnic group.

I have interviewed offenders who grew up in extremely impoverished conditions. In nearly every case, they had brothers or sisters who grew up in the same home and in the same neighborhood, but they did not turn to crime. Over the years, what has impressed me most is not the circumstances in which people grow up, but the choices they make while coping with those circumstances. The environment can provide fewer or greater opportunities to commit crimes. In neighborhoods where firearms and drugs are as easy to obtain as cigarettes, most residents shun both. Focusing on the larger social environment tells us almost nothing about the individual, only about the challenges which he or she faced.

There are aspects of a person's character that come to light in one environment but remain hidden in another. In the competition for admission to highly selective colleges, pressure to excel is intense. Consider a classroom of high school students taking a history final exam at the end of the critically important junior year. Some youngsters will not cheat because they are supremely confident of their mastery of the subject. Some students are so repulsed at the very thought of cheating that they would not cheat even if there were desperate. It is not just a fear of getting caught that deters them. Cheating is out of the question because it runs contrary to their values. Other students have few qualms about cheating, because their attitude is that any means to an end is acceptable—do whatever it takes! Where the environment might make a difference is with students who are tempted to cheat but hesitate until they have scanned the room to see how closely they are being monitored. If there is little oversight, they may consult a cheat sheet or glance at another student's paper. If a proctor is closely monitoring the exams, they play it safe rather than risk discovery and punishment that might cause them to lose credit for the entire exam or incur an even more severe disciplinary action.

There is also the person who stares blankly at an exam and, out of desperation, cheats. Even though he gets away with it, he is so uncomfortable about what he has done that he never cheats again. Years later, he still experiences a flash of guilt when he thinks about having succumbed to temptation that one time. For that individual, no *pattern* ever developed. Cheating never became "in character."

To the extent that cheating becomes habitual, it can inform us about a student's character. The environment does not "cause" a person to cheat; it can provide an opportunity for that element in his character to surface.

The same can be said of people who cheat on taxes. Some men and women are meticulously honest in filling out tax returns. This may be because they fear an audit and the penalties for cheating. Or it may be because they have a strong conscience. At the other extreme are taxpayers skilled at defrauding others. They believe what applies to others does not to them. Recall hotel magnate Leona Helmsley stating with contempt, "Only little people pay taxes." Mrs. Helmsley went to prison, demonstrating that she wasn't as smart as she thought. Between the extremes of the 100 percent honest taxpayer and the regular tax defrauder are others who, occasionally (again the concept of a continuum) cheat on taxes by inflating deductions or underreporting income. Environmental conditions may play a role in a person's deciding whether to cheat. If the word is out that the likelihood of an audit is minimal because the IRS is bearing down mainly on businesses, he may be more likely to cheat than if he thinks the IRS will crack down on individual taxpayers. Environmental conditions may figure into the calculation, but they do not "cause" the dishonest behavior. The individual makes the choice!

I have evaluated men, women, and children who have committed an array of property crimes, violence, sex crimes, and alcohol- and drug-related offenses. Their crimes appear in stark contrast to the way others describe them. A serial rapist was lauded by his brother as "honest, vulnerable, quiet, and unassuming." A mother of two young children who murdered her husband had no criminal record. A friend praised her as a generous person who was "always willing to help" and who never uttered a curse word. A highly educated, well-mannered aficionado of classical music sexually molested young boys. He too had no criminal record. A shocked friend characterized him as "a decent man who did an indecent thing." A young man who murdered his mother was described by a friend as "putting women on a pedestal" and loathing anyone who uttered an unkind word about his mother.

If you believe that the fruit does not fall far from the tree, you may be wondering about the parents who raised these men and women charged with committing such serious crimes. What traumatic or pathological events occurred during childhood that may have had a critical, perhaps traumatic, impact on them? Much attention has been focused on the family background of people charged with serious crimes, even to the point that some jurisdictions have held parents legally responsible for their offspring's criminal activity.

Psychology, psychiatry, social work, and education have long promulgated a deterministic view that children enter the world much like unformed lumps of clay. That clay is then molded by the environment, parents being the most influential. However, childrearing is not a one-way street. From birth, children differ in temperament. Babies differ from one another in their level of activity, alertness, fearfulness, and sociability. A mother or father responds differently to an "easy," cooing, content infant than to a "difficult" or cranky, colicky infant. The child shapes the parent's behavior as well as vice versa.

Let's look at one example of the conventional wisdom that adheres to the lump of clay philosophy. Many offenders have told me that they were abused by one or both parents. There is a voluminous professional literature that asserts that offenders "abuse" others because they were abused as children. A number of problems are inherent in what has been called the "abuse excuse" invoked from time to time in criminal cases. Criminal defendants are not usually truthful. They may claim they were abused when it never occurred. Children respond very differently to abuse when it actually occurs. Reactions include anxiety, social withdrawal, self-blame, and, occasionally, increased aggressiveness. Although adversely affected at the time of their harsh treatment, they turn out to be remarkably resilient.[2] Many formerly abused children become stable, law-abiding men and women determined never to inflict upon others the cruel things that were done to them. You don't hear about these individuals on the evening news or read about them in the newspaper

Ben told me that as a child, he was locked in a room, tied to a bed, and beaten. He clearly was making a case that his ending up in jail was related to parental mistreatment. Asked if his parents treated his siblings the same way, Ben shrugged and replied, "Of course not! They weren't doing what I was doing." What was he doing? I interviewed his mother, who acknowledged that, as alcoholics, she and her husband had not been very good parents. Nonetheless, all her children turned out well except for this one boy whose lying, stealing, and bullying started when he was a toddler and just got worse over time. No matter what she and her husband did, nothing had an impact on Ben. Reacting to his worsening behavior, they became more punitive. Unquestionably, the other children experienced difficulties while being raised by two alcoholic parents. But they responded differently and, in turn, elicited different treatment by their mom and dad. Ben, the child who was the most difficult and an abuser of others, is presently serving a life sentence for homicide, while his siblings have been living productively and responsibly.

Numerous times, I have discovered that the abuser was not the parent, but the defendant. More than one parent has related that, no matter what she did, she was rejected at every turn by her offspring. Both mothers and fathers remember that devoting more time and attention to the difficult child was to no avail. They were spurned, reviled, and victimized. In some households, as a child the offender kept the family in a state of siege as he stole, snuck out, concealed illegal drugs in the home, terrorized siblings, and threw frightening temper tantrums.

Psychological determinism may be intellectually satisfying because it appears to provide insight into the causes of an individual's criminality. But seeking such intellectual satisfaction usually derails the quest to obtain an accurate understanding of the character of the defendant.

An evaluator cannot rely on family history to provide accurate insights into the defendant's personality. With blood being thicker than truth, I have found that family members are protective of the defendant even when he has committed an egregious crime, sometimes even when they are the victims. Parents often feel as though they are on trial, especially if they have been implicated by the perpetrator as the cause of his difficulties. Many mothers and fathers are overwhelmed with shame and guilt. They clam up for fear that they may be blamed further for causing or contributing to the defendant's criminality.

In a criminal proceeding, when family members, already under stress, are asked to reconstruct events, they are inclined to focus on the positive and either forget entirely or conceal what is negative. Family members walk a fine line as they are virtually compelled to acknowledge incontrovertible facts of a case, yet strive to preserve a view of the defendant that he is not ill-intentioned, dangerous, or evil.

In one case, a defendant confessed to having killed a mother and child during the course of a robbery. Family members testified that he had suffered a developmental delay, that he had grown up overseas in a war zone, and was not at heart a bad person. Although they were powerless to mitigate the horror of the crime, they did their utmost to evoke sympathy for the defendant, hoping that he would be spared the death penalty. The man received a sentence of life in prison.

Family members may be genuinely baffled as to why the defendant behaved as he did. For years, they may have witnessed behavior so perplexing that they came to believe that the individual was suffering from a mental illness.

In one case, I was evaluating Herb, a young man who stabbed his mother to death. Although I was appointed by the prosecution to conduct the evaluation, the defendant's father agreed to be interviewed. Despite the death of his wife to whom he had been married nearly 30 years, this grieving husband showed no bitterness toward his son but characterized him as a good boy who was descending into a psychotic state until he finally snapped and attacked his mother. I found Herb to be lucid, cogent, and rational. He laughed at his father's contention that he ever was psychologically ill. Herb described his father as a tyrannical megalomaniac who was physically and emotionally abusive. During the interview, the father came across as a highly educated, cultured man, and as a devoted and conscientious parent. Herb denounced both parents, asserting that they cared only about appearances and were mean to him because he didn't share their values and fit into their mold. As the evaluation proceeded, Herb disclosed the abuse that *he* dished out by assaulting his siblings and threatening his mother. Family members grew so dismayed about the path that he was taking that they consulted mental health professionals. Whatever the parents' flaws were, his sisters grew up in the same circumstances. Both turned out to be responsible and successful, only to be cruelly deprived by their brother of a mother whom they cherished.

Another problem in relying on information offered by family members is what I call the "circle the wagons" syndrome. Even in the most heinous murder trials, relatives portray the defendant in the best possible light. It is sometimes difficult to distinguish what family members truly believe as they testify with the aim of saving their offspring from receiving a lengthy sentence. Washington, D.C. sniper Lee Malvo's relatives testified that he was a neglected and abused child, a good boy until he got into the clutches of John Muhammad. However, one would not expect them to mention Malvo's dark side. Their testimony supported the view of Malvo as a victim of a bad childhood.

Sometimes family members are so shocked at what the offender is charged with that they don't know what to think. They cannot believe that the person with whom they have lived could have committed the offense. In a murder case, I was appointed by the court to assist the defense during the sentencing phase for Roger, who had been convicted of killing two people. When Roger visited his grandmother Alice, mainly on holidays, he was on his best behavior. Alice related that her grandson was so quiet "you didn't know he was in your house." She said she had never seen him become angry. Alice explained, "It was like he snapped. He's not himself." An uncle also spoke of how quiet Roger was, "never a talk back boy." Recalling Roger's visits on holidays and special occasions such as birthdays, the uncle said, "We never had a bit of a problem with him. I've never seen him really upset." With regard to his nephew being charged with homicide, he emphatically stated, "I'll never believe he did it."

My point is that it is difficult to obtain valid information as to what a defendant was like during his younger years. Understandably, most parents do not welcome scrutiny by strangers. Yet, most want to be perceived as cooperative. In an unusual case, Rick was certain that Adele, his sister, was about to be murdered by her fiancé. Rick responded by shooting and killing the fiancé. Adele and Rick had a close relationship. Adele's dilemma was that she did not want to disparage her deceased fiancé, nor did she want to further jeopardize her brother's legal predicament. Consequently, what she said during my interview was not particularly illuminating. Rick's parents were in an equally difficult predicament. They were apprehensive about how they might be perceived, since the crime had occurred while all of them were living in the same household. I developed an understanding of Rick's personality not from what his sister or parents related, but by spending hours interviewing him as well as speaking with several unrelated individuals who knew him well.

If I interviewed anyone, including you the reader, and you had followed a criminal path, I could find an adversity in your background that could explain why you committed a particular crime. For who has not encountered difficulties growing up? After the fact, a psychologist can apply his causal theories to explain anything. But in doing so, he is likely to be more clever than correct.

What it all comes down to is that ferreting out information about what happened to the defendant as he grew up often turns out to be a distraction from the task of unraveling the criminal mind. My objective is to establish what a hypothetical videotape would reveal about the way he has lived his life. The tape would show us everything exactly as it occurred without explanation, rationalization, or editing. If we had my hypothetical videotape, we would not see the "why" of anything—just how this individual lived his life, the places he went, the people with whom he spent time, and how he dealt with life's challenges and disappointments. Proceeding in this manner is far more fruitful than embarking upon an archeological expedition into the person's past to dig up causal explanations. Focusing on how the offender has lived day to day goes a long way toward developing an understanding of his criminal behavior and of the thinking that gave rise to it. Such an approach is likely to provide helpful clues to understanding the supposedly "out of character" crime.

The centerpiece of the forensic evaluation, of course, is the personal contact in interviewing a defendant who has everything at stake. Let's now turn to considering how he responds to my efforts to understand who he is.

NOTES

1. Clark, Ramsey. *Crime in America*. New York: Pocket Books, 1971.
2. Alper, Joseph. "When Bad Things Happen to Good Kids," *The Washington Post* (Health Issues), September 1, 1987, p. 7.

CHAPTER 6

Interviewing the Defendant: The Setting

T he scope of my task is to perform a "forensic" psychological evaluation. Forensic psychology is a specialty which deals with court-related matters that can be criminal or civil in nature. Examples of the latter are child custody evaluations or evaluations of individuals who are claiming psychological damage because they were crime victims or involved in an accident. To conduct a forensic evaluation of a defendant in a criminal matter, I interview the offender in depth, assuming he agrees to participate, which is not always the case. Once I was retained by the prosecution in a capital murder case to evaluate a defendant for the phase of the trial in which a jury would determine the penalty. The defendant knew that, unless he cooperated, his attorney would not be allowed to introduce psychological evidence at the trial. The man remained adamant and told me in no uncertain terms that he would not answer any questions.

Let's talk about how I happen to be sitting across a table about to interview a man or woman who has committed a heinous crime. I may be conducting the evaluation at the request of a privately retained or court-appointed defense attorney, who asks me to evaluate his client for one of two reasons. He hopes that my assessment will contribute to a favorable outcome for his client either during the guilt or innocence part of the trial or during the sentencing phase. Another reason for seeking my help is that the more the lawyer knows about his client, the better he can represent him. My report may inform and thus forewarn a lawyer of negative characteristics of his client which could become a focus when the prosecution presents its case.

I may be asked by the prosecution (called the "Commonwealth's Attorney" or the "District Attorney") to conduct an evaluation to determine the defendant's mental state at the time of the crime (for example, in an insanity defense). Or I may be asked to evaluate a defendant to obtain information relevant to the court's imposing a sentence. I may be asked about the person's likelihood to re-offend, the presence or absence of remorse, conditions necessary for community supervision, or a need for mental health treatment.

While obtaining information about the defendant, my role is that of a psychological sleuth. One never knows what may turn out to be a key piece of psychological evidence. Given that the offender is in legal jeopardy, he is likely to be wary of disclosing anything that might appear unfavorable. As I work to develop an understanding of who he is, I will have to penetrate layers of psychological defenses. It is important to my assessment to have access to people who know the defendant well— "collateral sources," as they are called—who have specific information or a perspective regarding the defendant. These individuals include family members, mental health professionals, teachers, employers, and close friends. Another component of the forensic evaluation is my review of documents pertaining to the individual's history, character, or state of mind at the time of the crime. I may review police reports, school and occupational information, health and mental health records, criminal records, or pertinent audiotapes and videotapes. In one case, I listened to a tape recording of a eulogy that a distraught man delivered in church during his father's funeral. The next day, he went on a shooting spree in his neighborhood. The issue at trial was whether he was legally sane at the time of the crime.

If I am assisting defense counsel, there usually is no problem in getting other people to talk with me. If I am appointed to assist the prosecution, there is an understandable wariness about participating on the part of family and friends. Nonetheless, some people agree to be interviewed because they think it important for a potential prosecution expert witness to have certain information. Usually, the information is offered from a viewpoint sympathetic to the defendant, but not always. In one case, a stepparent wanted me to know of the emotional and physical abuse dished out to her and other family members by the defendant when he was a teenager.

I have conducted evaluations in a variety of settings ranging from the relative comfort of my office to the starkness of a small, stuffy room in the bowels of a jail constructed 75 years ago. In most facilities, I am locked into the room with the defendant. (There is a "call" button to summon a deputy if I need assistance. I have never pushed the button for emergency assistance.) As we proceed, I do not write rapidly enough to take down every word, but my notes are voluminous enough to accurately reflect what transpires. Never has a defendant objected to my nearly constant writing. I think that is because they realize that I am taking what they say extremely seriously and am not depending on memory, which is unreliable. At the very least, taking notes indicates that I am paying close attention.

From the moment I meet the defendant, he begins casing me out. In fact, he may already have obtained information about me from his attorney or from other inmates. If he is not yet incarcerated, he may have looked me up on the Internet or even taken the trouble to read a book I have written.

At the outset, I must determine whether the defendant understands the situation he is in and why I am interviewing him. If I am privately retained at the request of his own lawyer (not appointed through the court), he is inclined to be more forthcoming than he otherwise might be, especially if he knows that my report will be utilized only if his attorney thinks it will be advantageous. If I am appointed by a court, I inform the defendant whether I am assisting the defense or the prosecution. I inquire as to whether he knows what he has been charged with, the possible penalty, who the attorneys are and what their role is, and when and where his trial will be held. I let him know that there is no confidentiality to our discussions and that both the defense and the prosecution will receive a copy of my report. I caution him that anything he says can be used against him in court.

Assuming that the defendant is competent to stand trial, meaning that he understands the above and has the capability of assisting his lawyer in defending him, we begin. We are each trying to get a "read" on the other. My manner is professional, cordial, and always respectful. By trying to set the individual at ease, I can eliminate unnecessary barriers to our conversation. I decline offers to have a third person in the interview room, such as a correctional officer. If the inmate is wearing handcuffs, I ask a deputy to remove them (unless I have reason to think there may be personal safety issues, which is almost never the case). Since each interview is usually between two and four hours long, I tell the defendant he can take breaks. If a question is unclear, he should request clarification. If he does not want to answer a question, that is his prerogative. Comfort is not to be ignored. One inmate whom I saw in jail looked physically uncomfortable, the way he was shifting around in his chair. When I inquired if something was wrong, he said his back hurt. I told him to feel free at any time to stand or move around the small interview room. He seemed to appreciate this but never left his chair. I think that just the knowledge that he did not have to remain in one place and endure discomfort was reassuring.

I must be aware of the defendant's efforts to protect himself legally and psychologically. For he is in a dilemma. If the defendant shuts down or becomes combative, then he does himself a great disservice. On the other hand, if he reveals too much, he risks having it used against him. Most defendants want to control the interview while they try to convert me to their point of view. There is a strong likelihood that the person I am interviewing will endeavor to appear cooperative, all the while resisting disclosing what he thinks may be incriminating events that my hypothetical 24-hour videotape would reveal.

Beginning with our first meeting, I can count on facing an array of well-practiced tactics that the defendant has utilized to thwart parents, teachers, employers, and others who have tried to hold him accountable for misconduct. He has deployed these tactics to throw others off the track so that he can be absolved of wrongdoing or, at the very least, minimize his culpability.

Michael was sent to me by his probation officer for a psychological evaluation of his current functioning and amenability to counseling. Convicted of a string of burglaries, he had served three years in prison with 17 additional years being suspended, provided he successfully complete five years of probation. Michael's approach was to give the appearance of cooperation while disclosing little of substance. Voicing his opinion that seeing me was a waste of time, he declared, "Everything is fine with me. I don't see any point whatsoever. If she [i.e., the probation officer] wants me to come every week, I'll come." He then proclaimed, "You can't legislate someone to do right." He asserted, "The less I say, the better off I am." His words proved prophetic, for he never was open in his communication. During 45-minute meetings, this man would deluge me with talk but disclose very little. He spent a lot of time complaining about his wife and co-workers but kept wriggling out of assuming any responsibility for creating the difficulties to begin with. He professed that because his top priority was to "stay out of trouble," he limited contacts with old associates to "hi and goodbye." Less than a year after being released from the penitentiary, Michael returned to using drugs and stealing. Again incarcerated, he began writing letters asserting he had changed and requesting I support him at his parole hearing— something I did not do.

Five well-practiced tactics were in evidence throughout my contact with Michael. It became evident that his intention was to appear compliant while trying to conceal evidence that he had resumed his former patterns of behavior. One tactic was Michael's calculating how much he needed to disclose in order to *feed* me what he thought I wanted to hear. He'd tell part of the truth, but omit the rest. A second tactic was deliberately being *vague* about his activities. Number three was *minimizing* the seriousness of his conduct. For example, Michael was doing a lot more with former buddies than saying hello and goodbye. Number four was persistent attempts to *divert* me from touchy matters so that he could avoid revealing anything incriminating. And a fifth tactic was to seize the offensive and *criticize other people* rather than permit discussion of his activities.

Let's now consider the tactics used by Elizabeth during my evaluation of her while she was in jail for killing her elderly landlady. After a fashion, Elizabeth answered my questions, but tried to create an impression that the landlady, not she, was the problem.

Question: "What was the arrangement between you and your landlady?"

Answer: "I needed a place to live, and she wanted $200 for almost nothing."

Question: "Is $200 a lot of money?"

Answer: "The prime fee in this area is $700 a month."

In this exchange, the defendant was disparaging of her living quarters. With follow-up questions, she acknowledged that she had a bargain rent.

Elizabeth complained that she and her landlady "got on each other's nerves." Her characterization of the landlady was that she was a miserable old crab with no redeeming features. As we discussed the relationship between the two, it became clear that the landlady was quite concerned about Elizabeth because she spent the day hanging around the house and refused to work.

Question: "What didn't you like about her?"

Answer: "She was very critical of people—a backstabber."

Question: "Did she criticize you?"

Answer: "She criticized me daily....She said I was laying around doing nothing."

Question: "What was your routine?"

Answer: "I didn't get up until noon. I didn't go out until 3:30....I'd sleep, walk around, write."

Elizabeth continued to portray her landlady as unreasonable, especially because she objected to a boyfriend coming into the house. When I asked Elizabeth about this young man, she knew little about him, not even whether he was employed. Asked if he used drugs, Elizabeth replied, "That's up to him to reveal. I know what he did with me." Elizabeth acknowledged she wanted to use her landlady's house for sex and drinking.

Question: "Did she let him come over?"

Answer: "She didn't even want me there. I get so angry every time I think about it...I asked if we could park a van there. She didn't want a man living there. She objected to his alcohol use."

As we continued to talk, Elizabeth unrelentingly portrayed herself as a victim of this elderly woman who was critical of the dissipate life this young woman was leading while living in her home. Elizabeth paid a law rent for which she was required to do very little in return.

Whatever was asked of her, Elizabeth ignored. (She commented, "I had a tendency to forget to dust.") Elizabeth was furious whenever the landlady tried to steer her onto a more productive path, whereas she preferred to laze around with her boyfriend.

Question: "What other things did she say that you had problems with?"

Answer: "She said she thought I ought to have to do community service to receive my [unemployment] check. She said God meant for everyone to work and to have no pleasure."

Question: "How did you respond to her community service statement?"

Answer: "I don't think I want to respond. I don't think it's worth remembering."

Question: "Did you ever like her?"

Answer: "No. She's a person who's destructive to the minds of decent human beings."

Question: "Why did you stay there?"

Answer: "I had no other place to live."

From this discussion, I quickly learned that Elizabeth bristled whenever anyone imposed limits or questioned her conduct. She was not receptive to well-intentioned advice because it ran counter to the way she wanted to live. The protective tactics that Elizabeth utilized were vagueness (about the boyfriend), a direct refusal to answer a question (regarding the drug issue), going on the attack by making another person (the landlady) the target, and presenting herself as a victim (i.e., of what she considered to be an unreasonable, demanding, nasty landlady).

You might think quite correctly that anyone in Elizabeth's situation would say whatever would show her in the best light. I am not faulting Elizabeth or for that matter any defendant for trying to obtain a favorable outcome in a legal situation. The point is that I must recognize the tactics that offenders use when they are held accountable. Otherwise, I may be diverted from my task. If I had permitted that to happen here, Elizabeth was prepared to go on for hours reviling the landlady rather than addressing what prompted the landlady to behave as she did. By putting the landlady on trial, Elizabeth would have disclosed little about herself.

By maintaining a focus on Elizabeth, I was able to find out how she provoked the landlady and then stewed for hours over the things the landlady had said.

Elizabeth considered moving out even if she had to live on the street. When the landlady grew fed up and asked her to leave, they quarreled. Elizabeth rushed out of the house, her mind churning with fantasies of retaliation. Still fuming, she shoplifted a knife and returned to the residence. Another altercation ensued and, Elizabeth recalled, "I hit her and tripped her, then stabbed her in the back until she quit moving."

Feeding a person what he thinks the person wants to hear, vagueness, minimization, diversion, and going on the attack are among the tactics by which a defendant attempts to hide information. Deployment of these and other tactics in and of itself provides information in that it reflects how the offender typically copes with others who want to know more than he wants them to know. I will discuss tactical maneuvers in more detail in Chapter 16.

At any particular moment, I am unlikely to know for sure whether a defendant is being truthful. I may become aware of a lie from sources of information other than the defendant. By careful probing along certain lines, I find that the defendant eventually informs on himself.

A young man accused of homicide was describing how he sunk into depression during his financial struggles. I was puzzled. I knew he was living with a relative and had no expenses for housing, food, or an automobile. He had a job but complained that it paid poorly. When I asked if there were a way that he could have earned more, he replied succinctly, "Work harder." With this answer, I realized I wasn't hearing the full story. Through follow-up questions, I learned that he could have earned considerably more money but didn't because he despised work of any kind and did the bare minimum to hang on to whatever job he had at the time. Because of his erratic work habits and bad attitude, he was fired and remained unemployed for brief periods. When I pressed him as to how he spent what he did earn, he volunteered that half went to drugs, boasting that he used only the "good stuff," not the cheap, adulterated street drugs. The full story was that this young man did not lack opportunities for earning more money. Because of choices he made, he was the cause of his own impoverishment.

In chapters that follow, I shall discuss in detail the process by which I delve into a person's life so that I can establish a context for the crime that others view as "out of character." My task is to find out who the defendant was *before* he committed the crime. I shall take you along with me as I develop an understanding of perpetrators who commit crimes that, as it turns out, are very much "in character."

CHAPTER 7

Homicide of a Husband by his Wife or Alter Ego?

*A*nna was living a rather unremarkable life in a small southern city. Her husband Don went to work every day while she stayed home taking care of her two young boys. Neither she nor Don had any problems with neighbors. They were law-abiding, and had no criminal record. Their families, friends, and neighbors were in for a shock when they learned that Anna had picked up a gun and pumped bullets into her husband. I was asked by the prosecution to conduct a psychological evaluation of this woman. It was a complete mystery to others as to why Anna killed her husband. I was soon to learn that no one would ever have imagined that she was capable of any violent expression of anger, much less picking up a gun and shooting anyone. Her mother said that, as a child, Anna was timid and bashful. She characterized her daughter as "calm, easy going, very loyal, loving, and generous to a fault." A friend of 20 years said that Anna was "friendly to whomever she met, always willing to help," and stated that she was "a good mother" and such a model of propriety that she would not utter a curse word. A friend of Anna's deceased husband spoke of her friendliness to everyone.

The woman who sobbed hysterically while she was on the phone to 911 was not the Anna whom others knew. The police never had reason to come to her home. She had never set foot in a courtroom. And she had no history of consulting anyone for mental health treatment. To the

911 operator, Ann maintained that shooting Don was an accident that occurred during a very intense argument. Anna confided to the 911 operator that she had become so distraught that she wanted to be shot, but not to shoot Don: "He told me he said he hated me. I just wanted to shoot myself, and I told him to shoot me, and it just went off...I didn't know I shot him. I didn't mean to. I didn't know the gun was loaded."

Arriving at her home and discovering the dire emotional condition she was in, the police transported Anna to a local hospital, where she was immediately admitted as suicidal. On a Temporary Detention Order, Anna was held, then later transferred to a state psychiatric facility where she was evaluated.

Anna's attorney filed an insanity defense, maintaining that she acted on "irresistible impulse" after suffering a "dissociative" episode during which she believed that it was not she, but Samantha, an alter ego, who had pulled the trigger. A dissociative disorder, according to the American Psychiatric Association, "is a disruption in the usually integrated functions of consciousness, memory, identity, or perception."[1] One type of dissociation involves a "Dissociative Identity Disorder," formerly called "Multiple Personality Disorder." It is "characterized by the presence of two or more distinct identities or personality states [that]... recurrently take control of the individual's behavior."[2]

While at the state hospital, Anna told the psychological examiner for the defense that "Samantha" had been her imaginary friend and confidante since childhood—"the only one I could talk to." Anna said that Samantha had changed by becoming "devious and sneaky," dedicated to "keeping me in trouble." Anna asserted that this alter ego turned into such a pernicious influence that there were times Samantha would completely take over her personality. Then it would be Samantha who was in the driver's seat making decisions.

The defense mental health expert found that on the day of the homicide, Anna was suffering from a dissociative state. Her alter ego, Samantha, was in charge and was determined to rid Anna of all abusive males in her life. (Anna alleged that her husband was an abuser.) Psychologically, at that moment, Don was not her husband, but a target for Samantha to destroy. It was Samantha who aimed and fired, but the only visible person left holding the gun was Anna, for no one could see Samantha. Anna, extroverted, loyal, friendly, and a devoted mother, never was homicidal or suicidal. What transpired was all Samantha's doing. Anna contended: "They think I wanted to kill myself. I don't. I never have. Samantha wanted to die, not me...Samantha loves to ruin my life. I need to become me and try to leave Samantha."

I spent 13 hours interviewing Anna, who no longer was in a hospital but incarcerated in the county jail. In addition to information that Anna provided during the evaluation, I had access to a number of sources— her notebooks and diaries, police reports, psychiatric hospital records, and relatives and friends of Anna and Don who were willing to speak with me.

I had a lot to figure out. Staring me in the face was the obvious question as to how a nonviolent, law-abiding person had it within her to murder her husband. This became complicated by the psychological question of whether Anna could be held legally responsible for what she did. Did she murder Don, or was it an act by a part of her personality over which she had no control? Did she in fact have a "dissociative" reaction in which she was not aware of what she was doing?

When I first interviewed Anna, she apologized for her appearance and said she didn't have a mirror. From the moment of introduction, it became clear that this woman wanted others to like her and find her physically attractive. Whereas this is not unusual in daily life, it is not the way interviews in jail customarily begin. She said she had been reading the Bible and badly needed someone to talk to. Within the first 15 minutes, Anna indicated that she knew precisely what she had been charged with and stated that my job was to "evaluate my case, my not guilty by reason of insanity case."

Often I do not discuss the crime with which the person is charged until after I have had one or two interviews. This is for several reasons. All too eager to convince me of his point of view right off the bat, a defendant may try to submerge me in his self-serving account, employing a barrage of rationalizations. Or he may become fixated on rehashing the details of the crime, making it difficult to move on to discussing other aspects of his life, which he either doesn't want to get into or thinks is irrelevant to his case. If he succeeds in these maneuvers, I may learn about the crime, but very little about the person who allegedly committed it. Furthermore, deferring discussion of the crime may reduce the person's defensiveness. He may speak with me more readily and openly about a variety of subjects than he will about his conduct that has landed him in his current precarious legal situation.

Anna never showed remorse about Don's death. She had little positive to say about their relationship. Anna was disparaging of her husband, whom others characterized as level-headed, diligent at his job, a loyal family man, and stable in all respects. Ann decried his bad habits and claimed that he would stay out at night gambling and drinking. Yet, almost in the next breath, she'd describe him as a homebody who would disappear into the basement wanting nothing more than "his peace and quiet." Anna complained that Don had his "cruel ways" and never appreciated all she did for him. She criticized his watching X-rated films and claimed that he tried "to force himself on me." Anna said that after this occurred, nothing was the same ever again. So she sought out, as she put it, "my own escapes."

I thought that the topic of Anna's escapes held promise. Instead of sticking with the subject of the marital relationship, to which I knew we'd inevitably return, I was ready to delve into this subject that she introduced herself. To open the door to a flood of information, all it took was a simple follow-up question—"What sort of escapes?"

The first escape that Anna brought up was satisfying her voracious appetite for shopping. Anna amassed "boxes and boxes of shoes," heaps of jackets, coats, more than 100 winter shirts, and numerous other items. She commented that she hardly ever wore anything that she purchased. And she didn't even have to leave the house to indulge. The Home Shopping Channel was on 24 hours a day. "I'd wake up in the middle of the night and put it on," she recalled. The excitement was not in selecting the item or placing the order but in "waiting for it to come." Much of what Anna bought, she gave away. She said, "I shopped and shopped. I probably have $50,000 worth of credit card bills – stuff for the house, lots of shoes. I loved buying presents. I'd get high on shopping. Don would fuss. I'd hide it. I'd say I spent $200 when I spent $600."

Even though Anna was incarcerated, she had not ceased buying for the sake of buying. She said that at the jail's canteen she would "go crazy" and purchase "lots of stuff" including food and give it away. Anna made it clear that the next best thing to actual shopping was talking about it, and this she was prepared to do endlessly. When I thought we had exhausted the subject and suggested that we talk about something else, Anna remarked with a sense of relief, "Good! It's too exciting."

It was becoming evident that behind the image of the dutiful housewife and mother, this woman was a spendthrift and a liar. Many people shop their way into debt but they do not kill anyone, even the person who confronts them forcefully about their profligate spending. However, if one looks at what was going on with Don and Anna, a pattern was being established, which eventually started fraying the bonds of trust. Don worked long hours and tried to be frugal. As quickly as he was earning, Anna was spending money on items that she didn't need or use. She began hiding the mass of merchandise that she accumulated. Not one to micromanage his wife's affairs, Don entrusted to her nearly everything having to do with home and the children and seldom questioned what she did. Only after receiving mind-boggling bills in the mail did he become upset and realize that he had to do something to put a stop to their mounting debt. Trying to discuss finances with Anna was futile. She rationalized, justified, pleaded, and promised to reform. But her spending continued unabated until Don closed the credit card accounts. Then Anna used an ATM card to obtain cash, which she quickly spent. Her husband then stopped depositing funds to the account tied to the ATM card.

Upon learning that Anna had her shopping wings clipped, I figured that she had found a substitute. So I inquired, "When you couldn't shop anymore, what did you then do all day?" Without hesitating, Anna spoke in detail about her immersion in the world of the Internet, which she called a "pacifier." Like her shopping, spending time on the Internet became consuming as she found strangers available 24 hours a day to chat about all sorts of things. After spending most of each weekday tapping away on the computer, in anticipation of Don's coming home from work, she'd frantically rush around trying to impose order on the chaos created by the children and her own slovenly habits. "I'd go on this binge, and get rid of the clutter. I'd cut off the Internet and get into a cleaning phase. I was hooked on it like my shopping."

At night, while Don slept, Anna was on the Internet using two different names, her own and that of Samantha. Whereas she would talk to some people about family matters, the far less inhibited Samantha was interested in more racy subjects and delved into intimate and outrageous "cybersex" contacts. Anna, who wished to appear modest and demure, explained that, with Internet discussions, "It'd get to the point where Anna didn't exist. I'd be thinking I was Samantha." In other words, Anna didn't have the sexually explicit discussions; Samantha did.

With Anna's admissions of being virtually addicted to shopping and Internet use, I decided to determine what else she had been hooked on. A natural question was to inquire whether she had used drugs. One thing about Anna—she liked to talk! Nothing appeared out of bounds as a topic of conversation. Sometimes, however, she'd drown me in words without saying much. As I was to realize later, she was lapping up the attention I was giving her! Anna acknowledged dabbling in marijuana use, something she didn't particularly enjoy. But cocaine was a different matter. Anna volunteered that coke offered a feeling of power and excitement similar to shopping—"a good feeling, like I could do anything." Wanting to get married and to have children, Anna resolved to put drugs behind her.

Whereas she clung to her mother as a young child, Anna's shyness seemed to vanish when she entered high school. Anna said that before getting into drugs, she and her friends hung out and got drunk. She recalled sneaking liquor from her father's cabinet. Bored with school, she and her friends skipped classes with little worry about the possible consequences. Anna remarked that the school principal was good-looking, so she didn't care if she got sent to him for disciplinary purposes. If Anna liked a subject, she got A grades; if not, she would barely pass. Despite her erratic academic performance, she did manage to graduate from high school. Quick to make observations about herself, Anna acknowledged, "I've always been about getting my own way." The worst thing that she recalled doing as a teenager was to skip school and take off with a friend for five days to Florida. "I'll never forgive myself for doing that to Mama," she commented.

I was gradually learning more about Anna's sneakiness, her pursuit of excitement by doing what was forbidden, and her determination to do what she wanted, ignoring consequences. This information began emerging with what seemed at the time to be an innocuous discussion of shopping.

At the start of my second interview, Anna told me enigmatically that the defense psychiatrist had upset her mother when he asked her "about the man who messed with me." When I asked what that meant, Anna said that, as a little girl, she had been sexually abused by a friend of her father. She said that this was when Samantha entered her life: "That's when I first needed my friend."

Throughout the evaluation, Anna contrasted her personality with that of Samantha:

I'm afraid of everything. She's not afraid of anything. She was talkative, outgoing. I'm more conservative, quieter....Samantha was sexier, sexy and flirtatious, and I'm not like that....Samantha liked to live danger-ously, and I don't. I like to keep to myself pretty much.

Anna said that from early childhood, Samantha shored up her confidence, helping her to be strong. From then on, she depended on Samantha to advise her "like a sister." I probed in order to determine how strong this dependence, if it existed at all, became. Asked if she did everything her alter ego Samantha advised, Anna said not always. For example, Samantha directed her not to cut her hair, but she did anyway. Samantha told her not to get married, but Anna defied her. Anna proclaimed that Samantha's main focus was sex—"to have sex with anybody." This, Anna remarked, was in contrast to her own more reticent personality: "I wasn't a sex freak like she was." While complaining about the havoc that Samantha had created in her life, Anna told me that she missed her and wanted her to return. It was Samantha who made life exciting.

The most important thing about Samantha was that she was the one who did things that Anna wouldn't do. Anna attributed most of her irresponsible activities to her alter ego, even some of the shopping. At times, it was not clear whether Ann was talking about her own activities or about the nefarious conduct of Samantha. Asked who was doing the incessant shopping, Anna said, "Maybe it's both of us shopping together."

When it came to sexual intimacy, it turned out that Anna was not as reticent as she might have one believe. Her deceptive practices were not limited to shopping and Internet use. Anna offered a sympathetic ear to a neighbor who was confiding problems he was having in his marriage. Anna, not Samantha, had "a little fling" with him. When Don found out, Anna left the marital home for two weeks but returned when he threatened to take custody of the children. After yet another strain in the marital relationship, they reconciled, and life went on.

The night preceding the homicide, Don came upon photographs of a man nude from the waist down. He thought the photo was of the neighbor with whom Anna had the affair. She dismissed the photo as a joke and explained that it was actually of a different fellow, a "pervert" neighbor who liked to stand in his window exposing himself. When Don went to work the next day, he was still upset. Upon returning home that evening, he again brought up the subject and they argued heatedly.

Accounting for what transpired, Anna focused on Samantha's role, claiming that, two weeks earlier, Samantha had loaded the gun.

I didn't realize it was loaded. It wasn't me. You don't understand. She was going to kill herself. She ran back there and got the gun. Don said "what are you doing?" Samantha said, "Killing myself." Don said, "Go ahead." The gun was pointed toward him. . . .I really don't know what happened that day. All of a sudden, it was Don who was shot. . .It was Samantha's fault about Don!

I asked Anna why Samantha, whom she characterized as the happy, high flying sexpot, would be so despairing that she'd want to kill herself. Anna replied, "I'm really lost," and then urged me to talk to Samantha. Asked why she told the police on the phone that she shot Don, Anna said, "I was the only one there."

What I had learned thus far was that behind the image of the proper, demure, churchgoing housewife and mother, was a woman who had been an irresponsible excitement seeker since she was a teenager. A truant, a drug user, and a heavy drinker, she increasingly demanded that others accommodate her rather than that she fulfill the requirements of others. She got a thrill out of her clandestine shopping. Then it was the Internet that offered kicks. Anna contended that it was not she who was getting the thrills from the sexual repartee and that it really wasn't she who was living the high life. Rather, it was Samantha. It seemed that almost anything bad that Anna did, she invoked Samantha as the culprit. I realized that I needed to find out precisely what Anna herself was doing during the hundreds of hours that she, not Samantha, spent on the Internet, an activity that became so pervasive that she barely functioned anymore as a wife and mother.

Whereas Anna ascribed the flirting and graphic sexual banter with strangers to Samantha, she acknowledged that she participated in plenty of it. She vividly described cybersex and remarked, "You get into it and can really make it good." I already knew that Anna did little in moderation and would do things just for the excitement, regardless of the cost or whom she affected. No longer was Samantha the only one involved in sex on the Internet. Anna acknowledged, "I did it some; it was kind of exciting, something different." She said that she wanted to be more venturesome sexually, but after Don discovered her affair, she was reluctant to seek out an actual person for sex. So the Internet offered vicarious sexual excitement.

Anna said she liked looking up diets, fads, beauty pageants, and contests that she'd enter to "win free stuff." She acknowledged participating in cybersex with one man, while listening to the sexual fantasies of another. Anna volunteered that every day, she went online to "Married but Flirting," where she got to know 25 regulars. Some of the most graphic sexual talk she attributed to Samantha. But she was not consistent. At one point while talking about this, Anna announced, "I am Samantha." Toward the end of one interview, she began to get inappropriately coy and personal with me and commented about our interviews: "At least I get to see a man!" Possibly because she saw my wedding band, she asked, "Do you have any children?" and then, "Did your wife come with you?" With a smile, Anna inquired, "Do you want some company tonight?" Immediately, she followed this by saying: "That's why Anna doesn't like me. I get her in trouble. You can pick me up at the jail at 8 o'clock."

As one of the interviews concluded, Anna decided that she needed to instruct me how to banish Samantha so I would be certain that I was talking to her instead. She suggested, "Ask me about my kids. You can get me back."

When I asked whether the deputy would escort Anna or Samantha back to her cell, she answered, "Anna." However, still assuming the persona of Samantha, she said that she hoped Anna would return because Samantha "doesn't get along over there because there's not any man around." As Anna left with the deputy, she glanced flirtatiously at me. During another interview, she did not invoke Samantha but flirted by asking if I would buy her a soda, then suggested I take her to a hotel and order room service. This was not Samantha, but the pure unvarnished Anna!

So what had I learned? Anything dangerous or harmful, Anna attributed to Samantha. Everything from her voracious shopping to the homicide of her husband was Samantha's fault. Anna even claimed, "I neglected my kids because of her." Taking Samantha with a grain of salt, I wanted to learn more about Anna. There were times that I was able to keep Anna focused on herself without dragging in Samantha. It then became evident that it wasn't the fiery, impassioned alter ego of Samantha who was engaged in all the mischief. Anna was not as straight-laced as she portrayed herself to be. She admitted her own engagement in "cybersex." Anna owned up to the one night fling and to having in her possession the sexually explicit photos of a male neighbor.

None of the above revelations necessarily explain her turning into a killer. Anna had no known history of violence. I knew that I needed to return to the subject of her marriage to Don. I told Anna that I had interviewed family members, including relatives of her husband. She responded by expressing her smoldering resentment, not just toward Don but toward his entire family. She confided that she "always felt out of place around Don's family." She maintained that Don tried to rub her nose in the accomplishments of his relatives and "made it clear his family was better." She said, "They all went to college. Mine didn't. All had good jobs. Don made sure I knew it...He liked to make me feel stupid and dumb because I didn't go to college." Anna said that "constantly, day in and day out," she felt put down, belittled and humiliated.

Anna said that Don kept urging her to see a psychiatrist and even offered to pay. She thought it was part of a plan to make her look crazy so he could assume custody of the children. But Anna acknowledged that she was devoting so much time to the Internet that her children became starved for her attention. And Don was getting more and more fed up— first the shopping, then the Internet, the filthy house, and the neglect of the kids. Yet Anna expected Don to just acquiesce, no matter what she wanted. But that was not what occurred. She said, "Every night, I'd set a table. He'd get his plate and go downstairs or say he wasn't hungry and throw it in the trash."

Sometimes, they quarreled so loudly that neighbors could hear them. Although Anna said that she was afraid of her husband, that "he'd shoot

me while I sleep," she never provided a single instance in which Don was
violent. The closest he came was pushing her during one of their altercations, to which she responded by hitting him twice. Pressed about why
she feared him, Anna was at a loss: "He might have threatened before.
I don't know why. It was just something I thought. Maybe, I was
paranoid."

After asking me, "Am I a cold-blooded killer?" Anna made an
admission. During one of their fights, she got so angry that she pursued
Don with a broom and attacked him with it, striking him "a couple of
times." Thinking back to that fight, she said, "I was so mad, I could have
taken a knife and killed him."

That day he made me so mad, I could have grabbed that knife and
stabbed him....It was the way things were. He'd say to his mama "ain't
had nothing good since I've been here last." She'd believe him, and she'd
send him home all these things. She was just like Don. Nothing ever was
good enough [for him]. There was always something wrong.

During another argument, Anna told her husband that she wished he was
dead. In this deteriorating marriage, violence was not alien to Anna's
thinking or her behavior. Samantha was never even mentioned in these
discussions. "I have a really bad temper. I'd get so mad and throw stuff
at him....I yelled a whole lot." Expanding on her point, she told me that
in a relationship before she married Don, she would become so infuriated
with her partner that she would "plan ways to kill him"

I had the opportunity to interview at length individuals who had
known both Anna and Don for many years. When I conducted these
interviews, I already had had some meetings with Anna, and was able
to contrast what others said with what she reported.

Her mother said that of six children, Anna, with her calm and easy
going personality, was the easiest to raise. She had no knowledge of Anna
drinking or using drugs. She was critical of Don for taking over and
controlling the money. But she didn't have any idea why he managed
the money. Anna didn't tell her about her extravagance that resulted in
amassing large debts. All her mother knew was that she bought nice
gifts for people and did all the Christmas shopping. And, as a mother,
she considered Anna first rate! As to what happened finally between her
and Don, Anna's mother surmised, "They were fighting and the gun

went off." This, after all, was a mother who was very upset by what had transpired and even now did not want to think ill of her daughter. She provided little useful information—an instance of blood being thicker than truth.

Art, a co-worker and long time friend of Don's, had learned a few things about Anna. Working with Don for many years, he was privy to information that perhaps no one else knew, and, devastated by Don's death, he was more than ready to speak candidly. "Something about her didn't click with me," Art commented,

She was pretty sharp. She never had to work. Don complained about her spending. She knew how to spend it, but not make it. It got out of hand... I think Don really wanted to see the marriage work for his kids. The harder he tried, the worse it got...I thought she was a user.

Art said that it was "a known fact" that Anna was sleeping with the young man next door, known, that is, to everyone but Don. Art remarked that Don had considered leaving Anna but wouldn't do it because of the children. Sympathetic, Art even encouraged his buddy to "get a girlfriend on the side." Don wouldn't entertain that thought for a minute. Art said, "He was a hardworking man with a heart as good as gold. He'd give you the shirt off his back...The man stayed dedicated to his kids. He added on to his house so the kids would have their own rooms."

Ted was the infamous man next door. He told me that he knew all about Anna's talking dirty over the Internet. He had done the same. He explained that it is not unusual for one person to assume different names because they do not want others to identify them. Aware that Anna went by the name Samantha, Ted said she never seemed confused about who she really was. He noted that the Internet consumed her: "The Internet took control of her life. That girl didn't hardly go nowhere. She got hooked."

Ted was the neighbor in the nude picture. He acknowledged to me that Anna liked looking when he'd appear naked in the window of his home and masturbate. He remembered that right before Don was killed, Anna seemed terribly distressed: "She came to the door and said 'Don's mad at me. He done found some pictures'...One of them was me when I loaned her my camera, a naked picture, the bottom half of me."

Ted had taken a picture of himself to give to his girlfriend but left it in the camera bag. He denied ever having sex with Anna. As to arguments Anna had with her husband, he said he didn't hear words, only raised voices. In the aftermath of the homicide, Ted was blaming himself and had become depressed. He wondered if Don would still be alive if "it hadn't been for that stupid picture," which he is convinced triggered the couple's final quarrel.

Two of Don's relatives, John and Diane, had little positive to say about Anna. Of course, I didn't expect to hear praise for the woman who murdered their beloved family member. Long before the homicide, John and Diane had become progressively disenchanted with Anna the more they were around her. Describing her as a person who talked to hear herself talk and as "not the brightest bulb on the porch," they found her shallow, materialistic, and more "like a kid herself" than a mature, responsible wife and mother. Although they occasionally detected "a nasty undertone" between Anna and Don, neither John nor Diane knew of serious marital problems and definitely knew nothing of Anna's infidelity. As they vented their understandable bitterness and anger, I learned little new about Anna. No one thought anything was wrong with her mentally. Calling her insecure, Diane noted that Anna was consistently "the same person." John said that Don would get frustrated with her spending "but never thought something was wrong with her." But these relatives only were around Anna at holiday family gatherings. Speaking with Don's relatives, I asked if they knew why there was a gun in the house. They told me that Don's father wanted him to have it for protection, because there were times he had to visit his job site late at night. Don had no use for guns, but he accepted one to appease his father.

More informative than talking with people who knew Anna casually or saw her infrequently were the observations of jail employees who watched her daily around the clock.

I heard the following:

- Anna talked about her husband, but never expressed remorse about his death;
- She never mentioned being two people;
- "She goes off when a man comes into the room—she wants attention";

- "She talks with plenty of sense, no problem communicating with other inmates";
- "She has acted out as though she wanted me to notice a suicidal cry for help";
- "Her worst problem is her desire to make us believe there's something wrong";
- "I don't see any changes in her behavior that show she doesn't have her mental faculties."

The deputies watched Anna become dramatic and threaten to hurt herself. Although she compelled others to give her attention, Anna did not injure herself except to make at most a superficial scratch. One deputy commented, "Everything was superficial. If she wanted to really hurt herself, she could." She never made such maneuvers in the presence of a particular deputy who had bluntly told her, "Anna, I don't want to hear it."

As I compared what she had told her defense team with all I had learned during my evaluation, I questioned many of their conclusions. When she was first admitted to the hospital, Anna was observed to display "psychotic symptoms." Yet not one person who knew her for years before the homicide nor those who observed her in jail for weeks at a time ever saw any indication that she was not in touch with reality. The version of the crime she gave to the admitting physician was at odds with anything she said before or after: "The gun was too long. I put it under my chin and it wouldn't fit. So I handed it to Don so he could do it."

This was different from what she said to the 911 operator, to me, or to anyone else. Anna was noted to have "memory impairment." Yet her memory for details even of what she shopped for was sharp. I found no evidence of memory difficulties. A psychiatrist who interviewed her less than a week after her arrest reported, "She was able to provide her medical-surgical history appropriately and also cooperated with the mental status examination." Whereas at times she mumbled and stared in different directions, Anna did not appear depressed or guilt-stricken. The psychiatrist wrote, "She will need further observation to rule out malingering [i.e., faking] or a brief psychotic reaction." Finding no indication of a psychotic illness, he wrote, "Judgment is unimpaired." He did not find her suffering from a significant mental disorder, only from an "adjustment disorder with anxiety." A clinical psychologist found her competent to stand trial. (This was all before the defense mental health expert found her to be suffering from a mental illness.)

Anna had told me that Samantha appeared at the time she was sexually abused during childhood. She said no one knew about the abuse except Samantha. Yet, she told the psychiatrist that her childhood was normal and then denied any sort of abuse occurring, including sexual, physical, or mental abuse. She told an attorney that she had been raped as an adult, but never related that to me or any mental health professional. She told another mental health professional that she was raped as a teenager.

Clearly intent on establishing an insanity defense, Anna wrote to a doctor that she feared that Samantha might take over her mind forever. On one occasion, she wrote the doctor as though she were Samantha rather than herself, asserting, "I am nothing like Anna....I know she thinks I get her in trouble." The psychologist who wrote the final report for Anna's defense attorney stated that, at the time of the crime, she "was completely confused and disoriented as to who she was." Supporting a defense of legal insanity, he concluded that she was suffering from a "Dissociative Identity Disorder."

Putting everything together, I concluded that Anna did not suffer from mental illness, disease, or defect before, during, or after the crime. She had given a great deal of thought as to how to establish and fortify a defense of insanity and even discussed with me whether it would be successful. Since adolescence, she had sought excitement in doing the forbidden and illegal, including truancy, underage drinking, mind-altering drugs, racking up debt, marital infidelity, and spending days and nights in Internet chat rooms while neglecting her marriage, children, and home.

Anna had no history of mental illness. She did have a stormy relationship with her husband. More than once, she wished him dead, and in her mind she had killed him before the fateful day! As far as Samantha goes, Anna attributed any behavior of her own that got her into trouble to that alternate personality, assuming no personal responsibility for it. Her accounts of what caused the death of her husband were contradictory and, ultimately, she tried to blame Samantha. Even in confinement, Anna was observed to be manipulative, often dramatic, but always in control of her own behavior.

Anna's shooting of her husband was extremely baffling to everyone, even those who thought they knew her well. She had no criminal record.

She was known to be calm and easygoing, never violent. However, through hours of probing I was able to reconstruct her mental life to unmask who Anna truly was. I found the following thinking errors to be characteristic of her day to day functioning:

- A focus on herself to the exclusion of considering the impact on even the people closest to her, her children and husband;
- Deceptiveness to cover up wrongdoing (lies of omission and commission);
- A knowledge of what was right and wrong, but eliminating such considerations in order to do what she found exciting;
- Creating problems for others, then blaming them for her own wrongdoing;
- Concocting rationalizations for her own conduct when she was held accountable;
- An ability to shut off from awareness considerations of conscience long enough to do what she wanted;
- Dealing with adversity by fantasizing physically harming, then killing her husband, whom she regarded as the source of her difficulties.

Anna was a self-absorbed, controlling, deceptive individual who was determined to have her way no matter what. She dealt with what disappointed and frustrated her not with equanimity and creativity but by duplicity, vengefulness, and, ultimately, violence. Her shooting Don was very much *in character*!

NOTES

1. American Psychiatric Association. *Diagnostic and Statistical Manual of Mental Disorders*, Fourth Edition Text Revision. Arlington, Va.: American Psychiatric Association, 2000, p. 519.

2. American Psychiatric Association. *Diagnostic and Statistical Manual of Mental Disorders*, Fourth Edition Text Revision, Arlington, Va.: American Psychiatric Association, 2000, p. 529.

CHAPTER 8

The Defendant's View of Himself or Herself as a Good Person

When I was working in the Program for the Investigation of Criminal Behavior at St. Elizabeths Hospital in Washington, D.C., I was a neophyte. Just two years out of graduate school, I had never worked in a prison, jail, or in a forensic psychiatric setting. I gained quite an education during years spent assisting Dr. Samuel Yochelson, the founder and director of that program. Among so much new that I learned, perhaps the most astounding finding was that no matter how numerous, bizarre, or gruesome their crimes, every participant in that long term research-treatment study regarded himself as a good person at heart. As one man said, "If I thought of myself as evil, I couldn't live."

The defendant's view of himself as a good human being is an overarching theme that looms in every criminal case. It poses a challenge for an evaluator that is at least as great as the individual's precarious legal situation. Trying to evaluate a person while his freedom or very life is at stake poses a considerable challenge. As I have indicated, the defendant is faced with a dilemma. Refusing to cooperate usually is not to his advantage. Revealing too much has its perils. Whatever his legal status, I have found that each defendant is determined to convince me of his innate goodness.

I have heard defendants lament what they have done, tearfully acknowledge that they have hurt others, even agree that they deserve punishment. Nonetheless, they regard their crime as an aberration, a mistake, something that just doesn't reflect who they truly are. During interviews, they want the evaluator to understand that they are not "criminals" in the sense of mean, ill-intentioned bad guys. (Even in the rare instance when a defendant boasts about his crimes, that individual will claim to have a heart of gold.)

Anna (from the last chapter) wanted me to think well of her in all respects. Her first concern was whether I found her attractive. Not receiving the desired response, she turned to enlisting sympathy about having been trapped in an unfulfilling marriage. Anna volunteered that her husband was so insufferable that she was driven to seek refuge in massive shopping binges and in Internet cybersex.

Rather than providing evidence of her basic good character, Anna was acutely aware that these "escapes," as she termed them, would appear extreme and unsavory. And so she disavowed her personal involvement. It was not Anna, a dutiful wife and conscientious mother of two children, who was sexually depraved, much less capable of murder. The immoral and homicidal conduct was engaged in by Samantha, over whom Anna had no control.

Anna's cloak of self-righteousness developed major holes once I started interviewing collateral witnesses, including staff at the jail. While speaking with me, Anna was too clever for her own good and sullied her own virtuousness. She blatantly flirted but ascribed this conduct only to Samantha. She volunteered that she had a brief affair and that she had egged on a male neighbor into sexually exposing himself, then obtained a photograph of his genitals. Not for a minute did Anna say Samantha was involved in any of this.

As she repeatedly disparaged her husband, Anna gave herself away when she acknowledged becoming so enraged at him that she fantasized plunging a knife into him. Where was Samantha in all of this—her alter ego who came into existence when Anna was abused as a child, then remained in her life as a fun-loving, sexy, uninhibited adult companion? Since Anna told another evaluator that she never was abused as a child, I wondered if, in reality, Samantha was only an Internet screen name that Anna invented to hide that she was the one engaging in frenetic cybersex activity. Perhaps she invented Samantha in order to present herself as a good person during mental health evaluations.

There are various components in a defendant's view of himself as a good person. He may be talented and accomplished. He may help others who are less fortunate. He may be a community leader. He may attend church. No matter what immoral or illegal activity he engages in, a defendant is likely to draw a line between that conduct and other offenses that he deems reprehensible. A murderer proclaimed, "Anyone who messes with kids ought to be strung up." A teenage boy told me, "A person who knocks a little old lady down and takes her purse should be put away." Yet this very youngster broke into an elderly woman's home and terrorized and robbed her.

Most defendants know right from wrong (although in insanity cases this is the central point of contention). They are aware that people may be horrified by their crimes. Yet they readily admit that they would be irate if someone did to them or to a member of their family what they have done to others.

When the offender commits the crime, he is not thinking about whether it is right or wrong. This is because at that time it is "right" for him. One fellow explained, "I can make anything wrong right and anything right wrong. Right is what I want to do at the time."

To understand this more fully, it is important to know how offenders handle both the fear of consequences and the influence of conscience. The offender not only knows right from wrong, but he is very aware of the consequences that could befall anyone who engages in the type of offense that he is contemplating. He would be perfectly able to tell you that the person could get arrested, convicted, and sentenced to prison. If the crime involved physical risk, then injury or even death might result. The offender could relate all of this as it applies to another person. However, when *he* is actually committing a crime, he has a remarkable capacity to do something psychologically that most of us cannot do and have no need or desire to do. He can shut off consideration of consequences as quickly as you might flip a switch to turn off a light. He is sufficiently vigilant so that enough fear remains for him to look over his shoulder for the police or anyone else who might apprehend him and hold him accountable.

The offender also can shut off conscience. It is likely that, if asked a hypothetical question about people who strike women, he would not hesitate in expressing his loathing for anyone who would engage in such conduct. Yet, during a heated altercation with his wife over how much money she spent at the store, he knocks her to the ground. He remains a good guy, because of his beliefs!

This uncanny ability to shut off fear of consequences and to shut off conscience astounds most of us. How can a clergyman sexually abuse a parishioner? How can a dentist have sex with a patient while she is under an anesthetic? How can a woman entrusted with the care of an elderly patient betray her trust and rob her of jewelry she has cherished for half a century? The perpetrators of such crimes know that the acts they have engaged in are wrong. They vociferously condemn others who do the very same thing. Yet, when the crime was being committed, each of these "decent people" was able to eliminate deterrents from their thinking long enough to do what he wanted to do!

I do not take on directly the issue of whether the defendant is "good" or "bad." If I am perceived by the defendant as challenging his view of himself as a good person, I will have created an unnecessary obstacle for myself. For me to directly attack his perception of his inner goodness is to risk an early termination to the evaluation or perhaps getting punched in the nose (something that so far has not occurred). If the defendant senses he must defend his goodness, he may grow more guarded in his self-disclosures.

To clarify, I am not suggesting that every person who commits a crime is a "bad" human being. In any event, the issue is not what I think, but how a defendant views himself. The error is his failure to consider harm he has caused to his immediate victim and the damaging effects rippling out to many other people who were not directly targeted. The defendant's citing his positive qualities is a bit like a patient reporting he has perfect vision while acknowledging that he also has terminal cancer. The 20/20 vision is of little value!

Chapter 9

Pretensions

PRETENSIONS AND MURDER

A thinking error crucial to understanding the personality of offenders is their pretentiousness. Many expect to reap the benefits of success without doing the work that is necessary to be successful. They have an inflated self-image, which they expect others to affirm. When that does not happen, they become extremely angry.

Dressed in a suit, with polished shoes, an immaculately groomed man confidently strides into a store to be interviewed for a managerial position. He is already planning how to spend the high salary he expects to receive. Without prior experience or special skills, he is certain that he will impress the interviewer and talk his way into the job. Politely informed that he is not qualified, he is furious and gives the interviewer a piece of his mind. Another fellow, working in a restaurant, thinks that he is irresistible to women. Serving an attractive female customer, he begins fantasizing about getting her into bed. Handing her a menu, he flirts, certain that she will become so enamored that she will leave a generous tip and even give him her phone number. When she shows not the slightest personal interest and leaves a 10 percent tip, he follows her out and yells, "You forgot something" and flings the tip money at her.

Offenders who live in the world of their own pretensions are largely indifferent to others' feelings. They experience frustration and anger when others fail to confirm their view of themselves. The way that this mentality operates is that just thinking something makes it so. Because I am who I am, I deserve x, y, or z. The criminal is angry at anyone who does not hold him in the high regard to which he thinks he's entitled. This was precisely the case with Larry, who murdered his mother, the person whom he blamed for standing between him and a life of wealth and privilege, which he believed he deserved.

In his twenties, Larry lived with his mother, working in her home-operated mail order business. Although the business was growing, Larry immediately wanted an affluent life style, "high class" women, and respect in the community. Impatient and irritable because the profits were not what he expected, Larry wanted to manage his mother rather than have his mother manage him. During an argument about money and taking a trip, he strangled her, ending the life of the one human being who meant more to him than anyone in the world. Larry declared to police investigators: "I loved my mother with all my heart." In jail, Larry told me that he had always wanted to be "the perfect son." He said, "I wish it was me rather than her. I loved her. I never wanted to harm her."

Never denying to the police that he killed his mother, Larry said he had no idea why he did it. He remembered his mother snatching out of his hands the airplane ticket he had purchased and screaming that she forbade him to go to California and neglect the business. Larry retorted that she cared about no one but herself and her boyfriend, whom he detested. Larry recalled that, as their argument grew more heated, his mother picked up the business checkbook and smacked him on the head with it, whereupon he furiously turned on her. "I suppose I grabbed her around the neck and just kept choking her," he told me. Larry told police officers that strangling his mother to death was totally alien to his character. He sobbed, "Who's going to understand? I never hurt anybody in my life." He remembered that as a child he accidentally shot a bird with a beebee gun and never got over it. Recalling his sadness, Larry told me that he never again hurt another living creature. He declared, "I've always been the one to get hurt."

Larry appeared to be a young man pathologically dependent upon his mother, a woman who had severe problems of her own. He said that as he entered adolescence, his mother became increasingly overbearing. Despite having a boyfriend, she nonetheless resented his dating and demanded that he stay home to take care of her. She would throw a fit at the prospect of his being away, even for a night. Larry remembered his mother threatening to kill herself when he was to stay overnight at a school-sponsored activity. Larry acquiesced and did not attend. He told the police homicide investigator:

I've always been good to her. I fixed her lunch, breakfast, dinner. I've taken care of her all my life. I just finally recently got a life of my own....Every time I went out with my girlfriend, she got mad...She always threatened to kill herself. I just couldn't take it....I love that woman so much. I've always done everything for her. Everybody in the family always said I did too much, but I did it because I loved her...I hardly ever went out because I always worked for her...She was always threatening to kill herself. You know what it's like living [your whole life] with that?

Larry had reason to worry about what his mother might do to herself. She'd become so intoxicated and dysfunctional on alcohol or prescription drugs that he would have to put her to bed. On one occasion, she became so despondent and agitated that she overdosed on codeine and valium and was admitted to a psychiatric hospital.

At first, it seemed as though this was a case of a son so enmeshed and damaged by a parent that he felt he could break free physically and psychologically only by eliminating her from his life. Larry appeared, in a certain sense, to be a victim—a victim of his mother's mental illness. Having killed her, he lost the very independence he sought, for he would spend years behind bars.

While interviewing Larry for nearly 30 hours, I found that, although he portrayed himself as a victim, there was a lot more to the story. Larry had a difficult life residing with this deeply disturbed parent. However, I began wondering why he did not break away and leave, as do many individuals who grow up in adverse circumstances. Larry had a sister who had done just that!

Larry believed that remaining at home and enduring the vicissitudes of his mother would pay off handsomely. "I was going for the brass ring," he reflected. Before killing his mother, Larry believed he had already grabbed hold of the brass ring and was envisioning the grand success that he was certain was imminent. Larry already had identified the upscale community where he expected to live in style. He looked forward to becoming so well known and respected in his community that he would be elected to political office. Larry said, "I always had great expectations. We were coming up in the world."

If ever there were a case of pretensions outstripping accomplishment, Larry's was it. He had coasted through high school, barely graduating. He blamed his "C" average on the insatiable and unreasonable demands of his mother. When I questioned his claim that he had no time for homework, Larry acknowledged to me grudgingly, "Maybe I didn't have the getup and go." He saw little reason to attend college, commenting that he already knew more than most college graduates. "I know how to do anything there is," Larry declared. He had no job skills and no work experience other than the knowledge he had acquired through the home business. Despite his pretensions, Larry had no idea of how to live independently, for he never had to provide for himself. Only in jail did he start to take a look at himself and acknowledge, "I haven't accomplished anything."

Although Larry asserted that he was a prisoner of his maniacal mother, he managed to spend plenty of time with different girlfriends. At 18, Larry took off across the country with his 14-year-old girlfriend Sandra, with whom he had become sexually intimate. Sandra was having problems with her parents and was ready to leave home. The couple traveled nearly 1,500 miles and managed to survive an entire month until the police caught up with them. Larry was incarcerated, then placed on probation. Sandra returned to her family. Not long afterward, he spent time away from his mother, traveling to the West Coast. At the time of the homicide, Larry had a steady girlfriend whom he thought he might marry.

Citing F. Scott Fitzgerald's "living well is the best revenge," Larry insisted on living well immediately.[1] It started with females. He told me that he sought out girls with good taste and impeccable manners; only those from wealthy families qualified. With contempt, he asserted that he definitely wanted nothing to do with "bubble-headed, bleached blonds." Anticipating the life that he and his future wife would lead, Larry already had selected the prestigious private schools that their children would attend.

Leslie was one of the young women who satisfied Larry's criteria. As she became the love of his life, he doted on her and showered her with gifts: "I treated her like a queen. She wanted a life of leisure, and I wanted her to have it. I was extravagant. It made her happy."

Larry purchased diamond jewelry and a $200 bottle of wine. "I loved to see her smile," he explained. He also made a down payment on an automobile for Leslie and secured a loan for the balance using his mother's business as collateral. Larry commented, "I loved her; she needed it." Meanwhile, he did not neglect his mother, buying her expensive gifts as well. Larry commented to me, "I don't know how I get these girls. I'm no Robert Redford." He said that his girlfriends often told him he was "too nice."

Because he gave his girlfriends royal treatment, Larry expected to have them under his thumb. "I like subservient women," he remarked. Once these young women came to truly know the person bestowing the gifts, they became disenchanted. Rather than feeling grateful and obligated, they felt controlled and imprisoned. Larry said that three girls ended relationships by telling him off on the phone. Whenever any of these young women disappointed him, Larry felt victimized. He said about Leslie terminating their relationship, "She got the gold mine, and I got the shaft."

Larry became a serious student, not of academic subject matter, but of catalogues, books, and other publications depicting what he considered the good life. He devoured fashion magazines and books on how to dress well. He explained that having money assured power, prestige, and lots of leisure to do whatever he wanted. Regarding himself as a "person of worth," Larry read anything he thought "would make me a better person" or, as he explained, a person with "class." He said, "I didn't have the breeding like the Rockefellers. I had to learn it myself. I wanted to look the role, be the role."

Even though he lacked funds to invest in stocks, Larry started perusing the financial section of the daily paper. Intent on owning a mansion in a tony suburb, he subscribed to a magazine that listed premier real estate properties. He immersed himself in cookbooks and etiquette manuals, learning where to place a salad fork when setting a table, how to select wines, and which fashion designers were in vogue. He collected leather-bound editions of literary classics, explaining to me, "I wanted to start a library. I wasn't going to touch them until I had my own home." On his wish list for Christmas was a $5,000 Rolex watch.

Appearances were everything! Even the breed of dog he purchased was in line with the image he was cultivating. "Why did I get it? Because it was a snobby dog, a dog of royalty."

Larry believed that he already qualified as a member of society's upper crust. He questioned, "Why start from the bottom when you're several rungs up?" Larry was living the proverbial champagne life on a Coca Cola budget.

Larry commented, "My mother said I was living beyond my means; I didn't agree." Herein lay a major difference between mother and son. The former had an elementary school education, built a small business from scratch working night and day, and did not indulge herself with opulent surroundings and extravagant possessions. Unhappy as she was, Larry's mother endeavored to live within her means. This did not sit well with Larry, who remarked, "I wanted her to have social status. I taught her to dress properly and how to order wine." That Larry did not share his mother's propensity for frugality was evident when he admitted that he spent every cent as soon as he laid his hands on it. Flying to California for a vacation was one more thing that he couldn't afford, and his mother opposed his buying the plane ticket. Larry said, "I considered taking her with me, but I wanted to go alone." Even after the homicide, Larry said he wanted to retain the business "corporate name" with the idea that he could eventually turn the enterprise into a gold mine. "I loved that business," he told me. What Larry really loved was the prospect of the riches that the business might bring him.

As much as he railed against his mother's tyranny, Larry obviously saw her as his ticket to the good life. Money spent was not always money earned. An uncle commented: "[Larry] was extravagant. He didn't know the meaning of what money was worth. His mother gave him whatever he wanted."

The uncle recalled Larry's mother giving her son thousands of dollars in cash, money not earned for working at the business. No matter how much he had, Larry continued to incur massive debts. Unable to pay the bills each month, he also had to pay finance charges. After he was incarcerated, he received a bill from a health club for over $2,000. In reality, Larry knew nothing about managing or investing money. He was ignorant as to how unpaid credit card balances compounded. And he confessed that he hadn't the slightest idea how to fill out a tax form, for he had never done it.

Larry told the police about his fierce temper, indicating with a snap of his fingers how suddenly it can erupt. Larry argued frequently and vociferously with his mother, many times wishing her out of his life. Despite his belief that a gentleman never strikes a lady, Larry grew enraged to the point that he visualized slapping her. Both he and his mother were controlling individuals, both stubbornly insisting on their way. "Compromise is a weakness," he told me, and Larry obviously meant it. Larry wanted what he wanted, and no one was going to stand in his way.

Larry lived in a near-constant state of anger because of the huge gap between his pretensions and the reality he increasingly was forced to confront—the disappointing business income, the mounting bills and letters from creditors, the lack of what he considered sufficient appreciation from his mother, and the rebuffs from girls who grew sick of him. His mother's emphatic rejection of his taking a trip to California was the last straw.

Many people arrogantly live in a world of their own pretensions. However, they do not react to disappointment at others' failure to affirm those pretensions by taking someone's life. Larry's crime was not out of character. It occurred *because* of his character. Throughout adolescence and young adulthood, Larry's pretensions outstripped his accomplishments. He believed that only his mother stood between him and the privileged life that he thought he deserved. Innumerable times, he thought how much better off he would be without her. Larry translated recurrent thoughts into action. By murdering his mother, Larry annihilated the very person who gave him everything he had.

PRETENSIONS AND EMBEZZLEMENT

While serving as an employee in a publicly funded social service program, Fred was charged with embezzling to his own account payments made by program participants. His crime made local headlines not only because he betrayed the trust placed in him as a public official, but also because he seemed a most unlikely person to commit such an offense. Fred was an Eagle Scout and a college graduate and had no prior arrest record. A friend since college expressed the positive opinion of many who knew him: "This came as complete shock to us because it's just not within [Fred's] character to compromise the faith and trust someone has placed in him. And as for the illegality, this is inconceivable."

Fred was referred by his defense attorney for evaluation prior to sentencing. Fearful of going to jail and extremely apprehensive about what kind of future he would have if convicted of a felony, Fred seemed eager to speak with me. During the first interview, he acknowledged, "I've always believed the ends justified the means." He said that he had been successful in getting away with things throughout his life. When accused of wrongdoing as a child, he dissuaded others from punishing him with "an innocent look." He stole money from his parents on at least a dozen occasions before being caught red-handed. Although he had plenty of toys, he wanted to accumulate still more to show off to his buddies. While participating in sports, he would play unnecessarily roughly, pushing and tripping competitors. Fred aspired to be a million-aire by the time he was 30 years old, and his ultimate goal was to become President of the United States. Fred stated that, with a fierce ambition "to get to the top," he had "screwed over people."

A critical part of impressing others was to be seen with a good looking girl. He had a predatory attitude toward women in that he viewed them not as human beings but as challenges. "I go for looks," he said. Doing whatever it took to win their affection, Fred would demand an exclusive relationship. Once the conquest was made, he quickly tired of the person and moved on to his next prey. In a few weeks, Fred spent more than a thousand dollars on one young woman, a substantial portion of which paid for their hotel room rendezvous. After such extravagance, Fred would vow to be more frugal. That resolve lasted until the next female came along and he'd spend another fortune, only to dump the girl shortly thereafter. Fred manipulated women and went through dozens, growing attached to none. In the rare instance that a girl dumped him first, Fred took it very much to heart, recalling, "I'd feel the deepest hurt that bordered on mourning."

Fred appeared to have it all—intelligence, charm, a gregarious nature, and good looks. A heavy drinker, Fred became even more sociable at parties and bars. Now and then, he dabbled in illegal drugs, which he had heard were "supposed to help with sex." One person who had known Fred a long time commented, "He believed his own publicity," and observed that Fred was all façade and had little depth. Fred told me, "I can never let a mirror pass without a look." When he walked into a room, Fred expected to be the center of attention. With his titanic ego, he said he felt "easily slighted" when others did not respond to him as he thought they should. Inwardly boiling, Fred would contain his anger and try to appear impervious. Considering appearances all-important, Fred accumulated trappings of success, such as an expensive sports car, a boat, and a recreational vehicle fully outfitted for camping.

Larry and Fred were extremely ambitious and determined to have a life of great wealth and privilege. Both envisioned getting elected to political office. Many people with similar goals realize that achieving them is problematic. They understand that they must work hard, fulfill obligations, and cope with unexpected setbacks, and, overall, function with integrity. Larry wanted the family business to have explosive overnight growth to assure that he would have the life to which he believed he was already entitled. Fred expected to impress others so that he would quickly "climb the ladder" to success, becoming a millionaire by 30 and, eventually, President.

Both Larry and Fred clearly had an inflated image of themselves. Their pretensions were out of line with their accomplishments. Each took short-cuts, undeterred by moral or legal considerations. Expressing pity and contempt for people who struggle to earn a living, they considered them-selves above having to struggle. Convinced that they were smarter and more sophisticated than their contemporaries, they counted on securing immediate wealth and power.

Larry's mother became an impediment to his grand plans. Truly his benefactor, he regarded her as his nemesis. Despite a strong emotional attachment to her, Larry was enraged whenever she didn't capitulate to his plans, decisions, and whims. Although he did not premeditate the precise date, time, and place of her murder, he fantasized about a life in which he no longer had to put up with her. The day of the argument over his plane ticket, Larry liberated himself from her tyranny.

Fred had the same mentality, although the environment in which he lived was different. He worked in a government bureaucracy that was sloppy about monitoring client payments. Capitalizing upon this weak-ness, Fred lined his pockets with agency money, each theft reinforcing his sense of his own cleverness. The more funds he siphoned off, the more certain he became that he was on the road to the life he had long wished for and to which he considered himself entitled.

As I interviewed these two men, numerous errors in thinking became evident:

- Unrealistic expectations of themselves and other people;
- A failure to plan long-range;
- Hypersensitivity when they felt slighted by others;
- Self-centeredness to a point that they seldom considered the impact of their behavior on others.

But what stood out was an incredible arrogance and sense of entitlement that was not supported by their accomplishments.

Fred told me that he had come to realize that he had "an ego problem." Many people who are not criminals have a similar problem. They are self-centered and therefore difficult to get along with. Despite their self-absorption, their fear of legal consequences as well as their conscience deter them from engaging in conduct as egregious as homicide or embezzlement. Pretentiousness is a clue to character. It exists, as do the other thinking errors, along a continuum. During my evaluation of Larry and Fred, their pretentiousness nakedly emerged during the very first interview and continued to be a prominent theme in their thinking.

I interviewed these two men during a period in which they were despondent. This was a singular time in their lives when they were terrified about their immediate fate, which lay in the hands of a judge. They also were ruminating about their future prospects after they served their sentence. Fred said, "I don't think there is a rest of my life." He had contemplated suicide but said, "I don't have the guts to pull the trigger." Larry had told the police interviewer, "I just want to die!"

NOTES

1. F. Scott Fitzgerald, *Tender Is the Night* (New York: Bantam, 1962).

CHAPTER 10

The Self as Unique and Irresistable

RAPE

A prominent criminal defense attorney called me to evaluate a client whom he characterized as "an all-American kid who did a weird thing." Twenty-year-old Stuart came from a loving, stable family, earned outstanding grades, had a girlfriend, and aspired to join the FBI after graduating from college. He had no criminal record. Stuart was identified as the perpetrator of a rape of a teenage girl whose name he didn't know. After watching her get off a school bus, Stuart followed her in his car to find out where she lived. Sneaking into an open rear door of the house, he accosted and grabbed her, then tied a cloth over her eyes before raping and sodomizing her. As he was leaving, the victim managed to slide the blindfold down just enough to have a glimpse of her attacker. A neighbor who grew suspicious of a man sitting in a car idling its engine close to the victim's house jotted down the license plate number.

People who had known Stuart his entire life found it impossible to believe that he was capable of even contemplating such a crime. Stuart raked leaves, shoveled snow, and, in high school, worked part-time at a fast food restaurant, where he was considered the best, although the youngest, worker. An employer wrote in a character reference to the court that Stuart was "one of the most accurate cashiers we have ever had, and his honesty is beyond question." He added, "Any company would be extremely lucky to have him as an employee." The store manager predicted, "He will do well in any work he tries because he is very willing to work and take on extra responsibilities." Stuart's father said that he was proud of his son and commented, "I couldn't ask for much more." Shocked by Stuart's arrest, his dad declared, "This action is 99.99 percent out of character!" I was soon to discover that the rape that Stuart committed was actually 100 percent *within his character*!

Stuart's adoring parents, admiring neighbors and employers, and teachers and classmates had no way of knowing about a totally hidden dimension of his character. Entering junior high school, he refused to go to school dances and parties. He had the idea that girls wouldn't like him, that they would refuse to dance with him. As his peers had early crushes on girls, started having girlfriends, dated, and endured the insecurities and rejections that kids typically experience, Stuart remained on the fringes of the social scene. Rather than participating, he developed a secretive life in which he could be certain that he would appear irresistible to both males and females and always remain in control. He recalled that around the age of 13, he and a friend composed stories in which the protagonist would make sexual conquests. Stuart explained, "He'd write half a page, type it, give it to me. I'd read it and add on something else, then give it back to him." Every day after school, the two boys exchanged writings. Then Stuart pulled back from this activity because he didn't want his friend to discover his homosexual as well as heterosexual fantasies, most of which involved force.

As you learn more about Stuart, you may wonder whether, as a child, he experienced sexual abuse or trauma. If so, might that account for his violent sexual fantasies and the rape he committed? For decades, mental health professionals have promulgated the myth that perpetrators of sex offenders were victims who inflicted upon others what was done to them. This is absurd on the face of it. There is no evidence that most people who were victims of incest, rape, and molestation become victimizers. There are many responses to sexual abuse, among them social withdrawal, depression, guilt and shame, and anxiety. Many victims of sexual abuse resolve not to do to others what was done to them. Although they were affected by what happened, they show a resiliency and live productive lives without victimizing anyone. Stuart experienced no sexual trauma or abuse. At age nine, he and a friend fondled each other. When he was ten, he and a male teenage babysitter performed oral sex on each other.

To be sure, the sitter took advantage of the situation. However, Stuart remembered this as a pleasurable experience, not abuse. At 17, he had sexual intercourse with a girl. Thereafter, Stuart was never at a loss for opportunities for sexual activity. But consensual sex was nowhere as exciting as his own fantasies, which he savored and embellished over and over. In these, he was a sexual stud who imposed his will on males and females of all ages. While working diligently and impressing his employer, Stuart was fantasizing about a female co-worker. He remembered thinking that "somehow she might be attracted to me and we could have a relationship." Instead of putting this to a test by asking her for a date, Stuart learned where she lived, drove by her house a number of times, and stopped his car to masturbate, thinking about what he'd do to her. This way, he did not risk rejection and, in his mind, he could do with her whatever he pleased. On nearly two dozen occasions, Stuart followed other girls to their homes, parked in the vicinity, then masturbated. Central to his fantasies was a certainty that whoever he targeted would be attracted to him so strongly that she would submit instantly to whatever he asked.

Throughout adolescence, Stuart fantasized about having sex with male movie stars. "I'd invent some scenario where I'd meet them and get involved, like at a bar or in a park." Stuart thought about how these celebrities invariably would be physically drawn to him, and invite him to their homes where they'd have an orgy of oral and anal sex. Stuart spent lots of time and energy learning whatever he could about these young men. He pored over teen magazines, studying articles, statistics, and photographs. He pictured himself working in films, hobnobbing with the rich and famous, attending their parties, and going to gala premiers. He masturbated, fantasizing about "experiencing what they were experiencing."

Stuart indulged in other clandestine activities, which he found exciting because he was in control and no one had any idea of what he was up to. At ten, he stole money from his mother's purse, a little at a time, to pay for action figures. As a teenager, he stole from his father enough money to buy an expensive rock concert ticket. More than a dozen times, he shoplifted female clothing from stores and dressed up in it. Stuart and a friend alternated entering different stores to swipe Playboy and Penthouse magazines. At work, he wrote down a customer's credit card number and used it for phone sex. This was the beginning of a pattern of copying numbers from pornographic magazines and dialing for phone sex in which he was in charge and did not have to accommodate anyone else.

Earning outstanding grades in high school, Stuart was admitted to a prestigious college. Early in his freshman year, he seemed content with his surroundings and was performing well academically. He recalled, "Everything I liked—the food, the housing, and the weather." His satisfaction was short-lived because his girlfriend at home began calling him urging him to come home, because she wasn't sure she could remain faithful while he was so far away. Stuart's sense of security was shattered as she repeatedly warned that she had to move on with her own life. In relating this, he said, "I was really in love with her. It got me angry, frustrated, jealous all at once." One day he was so upset that he called every hour just to hear her voice. Convinced that life would be intolerable if he lost her, Stuart decided to leave school. He had to go home to get her under control: "I had to be there to keep her from going out with someone else."

Stuart rebuffed his parents' urging him to seek counseling. Contemptuous of counselors, he was positive he knew more than "the people in their little offices" who were ignorant about "real life." Rather than take a week off, as his father advised, Stuart withdrew from all classes and cancelled his housing arrangement. With no refund forthcoming, his parents lost thousands of dollars.

Once home, Stuart became even more distraught when he learned the full extent of his girl friend's activities.

She said she'd slept with 13 or 14 guys. Earlier on the phone she said two guys. It got me mad. She had been going out with her ex boyfriend [even while she and Stuart dated]. I was crying and asked her why. She said it didn't mean anything. . . . Just the knowledge tore something within me.

Stuart subjected her to an inquisition, demanding that she disclose specific sexual practices, then badgering her about inconsistencies in her accounts. Furious at her betrayal, he ended the relationship.

Sex was the one area of life in which Stuart expected to have complete control and to be number one. He wanted to be so adored and admired that others would unfailingly submit to whatever he demanded. This did not happen in real life, nor did it occur in the pornography that others wrote. And so he returned to his early adolescent pattern of writing stories. He could infuse into his compositions whatever he wanted and thereby orchestrate any kind of sexual situation. Until the police searched his home, no one knew that these writings existed. Stuart said about the stories, "They were just right at the moment for stimulation and masturbation." Their contents reveal a mind loaded with thoughts of rape. The stories depicted involuntary, always explicit, violent sexual subjugation of males and females as young as four, no older than 30. Embedded in one of the stories was evidence that Stuart was fully aware that there could be serious legal consequences to an adult having sex with minors and committing rape:

I know that most people would think this is a perversion of the worst kind, and that I would undoubtedly be sentenced to death, but hey we're all going to die someday aren't we? Yes, I figure that while I've got the time, why not use it.

Stuart wrote pages of detailed, graphic sexual scenes in which people are tied up, penetrated against their will, even threatened with death if they refused to submit to whatever he wanted to impose on them. "I wouldn't think about it; I'd write what was in my mind," he acknowledged. Anyone who read these graphic stories would have no doubt as to the cruelty and violence of the content. However, Stuart did not view them that way: "I'd make up a picture in my mind. There'd be some image of bondage, but I didn't look at them like force, but a willing party."

From Stuart's point of view, force was unnecessary simply because he was so desirable, absolutely irresistible. If a person submits to what one actually wants, it is not rape. The perpetrator is not a perpetrator, because he has bestowed upon the other person that which she actually seeks. Stuart wrote a story using the first person about being naked and having a ten-year-old boy stare at him "in amazement with his mouth watering." In another scenario, he described linking up with a twelve-year-old boy who instantly took to him and the two of them posed nude for magazines, becoming a duo for a centerfold, then traveling the world and posing nude for photographs. He treated both boys sadistically (e.g., tying up the ten-year-old and blindfolding him), but, from his standpoint, the youths had a pleasurable experience because they were eager for him to do what he did.

Stuart especially relished the idea of finding a sexually inexperienced young teenage girl who would be "curious and wanting to go through the sexual act and the pain." In one of his stories, he spoke of befriending an eight-year-old girl, then fantasizing how he would pursue and grab her: "She is screaming for me to let her go, but I only gag her mouth." Of a thirteen-year-old girl, he wrote, "I knew then and there that I would be the one to break her virginity one way or another....I felt like raping her right then and there." Stuart commented, "I had to experience it, to find out what the big thing was" in terms of being the first. This desire figured prominently in his eventual choice of the school girl as his rape victim. Stuart told me of his recurring fantasy: "She was somebody who'd fall in love with me somehow, just from seeing me. I was immediately attracted to her, that she was like a virgin, and I had to be her first. I had never experienced it." He said about the crime he actually committed, "The fantasy was coming real in front of me."

Awaiting sentencing in his jail cell, Stuart was able to describe the excitement he experienced at every stage of the rape. When he watched the girl alight from the school bus, he fantasized how he would feel "getting to know her." After a feeble effort to "put it out of my mind," he went full steam ahead thinking about her, "following her home and watching her." He had a sense of invincibility—"a mild form of feeling nothing can happen to me." He inquired as to whether she had ever had sex. When she said that she hadn't, he experienced strong sexual excitement, which he described as increasing at "the moment before orgasm and at the time of orgasm."

Psychological literature about rape ascribes the behavior to various causative factors—hatred of women, resenting one's mother, feelings of inferiority, and so forth. Thousands of men have difficult, harsh, abusive, or even mentally ill mothers, but they do not rape. Many men experience a sense of inferiority socially or sexually, but rape would not be something they'd regularly fantasize about much less actually engage in. Digging about in Stuart's past can only lead to confusion, explain nothing and, perhaps worse, offer excuses. Stuart had reason to resent his mother because she left the family for long periods due to conflicts with his father. But it was his mother whom Stuart wrote from jail, telling her how much he enjoyed his childhood, confiding what he learned about the dangers of fantasy, then telling her he loved her. He said to me about his mother, "I never had a problem with her. She was the person I was most open with." Stuart never attempted to blame any person or set of circumstances for what he did. Nor did I find anything about how he was raised during his formative years that shed light on the crime for which he was given a life sentence.

Achieving excellence in high school, being admired and praised at work, having parents who loved him, and an abundance of opportunities for the future were not what mattered most. Overshadowing it all was a secret life in which Stuart fantasized himself as irresistible to others and thereby able to control them. Stuart thought he could enjoy and contain that secret life. He reflected, "I'd console myself that I'd never let them get past being just a thought."

Millions of people view pornography in its myriad forms, especially on the Internet, where anything imaginable is available. During a pre-execution interview with psychologist James Dobson, notorious serial killer Ted Bundy deplored pornography's influence on him, how it shaped him into a killer of 12 females, one as young as 12.[1] He told Dr. Dobson that once fantasy no longer provided sufficient excitement, he acted upon his sexually sadistic and murderous thoughts. One wonders whether Bundy, who studied psychology at the University of Washington, actually believed this himself.

If immersion in pornography caused crime, the government could not build enough secure facilities to house the number of offenders there would be. People may energize their fantasies using pornographic materials. Some may spice up their sexual lives by trying out what is depicted on the screen or in publications. The use a person makes of pornography depends on his basic personality.

Stuart was accustomed to achieving whatever he set his mind to. He earned stellar grades, was admitted to the college of his choice, and received high praise from teachers and employers. Only with women did he lack confidence. To take control of a deteriorating relationship with one of his girlfriends, he abruptly terminated his college career and, in the process, caused his parents heartbreak while wasting thousands of their dollars. Returning home did not salvage the relationship. It was the one part of his life over which Stuart discovered he had no control whatsoever. To prevent further disappointment, Stuart could do what he did when he was much younger: rely on fantasy and have whatever he wanted.

Other guys had to take their chances with women. Not Stuart! In his imagined sexual scenarios, there was no uncertainty, not the slightest chance of rejection. Moreover, he need not rely on the pornographic creations of other people. In the fantasies that he wrote down, he was in a unique position of being an irresistible sexual attraction. He then could initiate any sexual act he desired with females or males who unquestionably would be eager to accommodate him. Stuart reached a point where neither others' pornography nor his own satisfied him He decided to live out his fantasies. While stalking women and secretly following them to their homes, he still could sustain the idea that, were they to personally encounter him, they'd be eager to do his bidding. Stuart hung onto the notion that the ultimate experience would be to find a virgin so he could be that truly unique person in her life—the first! The innocent adolescent school girl getting off the bus fulfilled his desire.

As I interviewed Stuart, I learned rather quickly about the details of the crime and of his immersion in pornography. He was ready to talk openly, because he was in jail and had been instructed by his lawyer to cooperate. As is often the case in such situations, Stuart held back something critical. He had told me about writing sexual fantasies with a friend when he was a boy. But his adult writings did not come to light until his attorney obtained a copy of them from the police, who found them during a search of Stuart's home.

The challenge is to place the crime in the context of a person's life. What sort of thinking patterns were embedded in Stuart's personality that coalesced and found expression in this horrible crime? Certainly, there are people arrogant enough to believe that they are God's supreme gift to the opposite sex, but rape is not on their mental horizon. Stuart had few close friends simply because he did not bother trying to make friends. Like many offenders, he thought he was unique in that he was better than others, singular in his capabilities, highly intelligent, and very accomplished. Stuart had social skills that were sufficiently adequate so that he did not appear odd or weird. He never experienced closeness or intimacy because he sat on a lofty perch, expecting others to come to him. If that didn't happen, it was not his problem. Others were missing out! Stuart's assumption was that a woman would be drawn to him, ready to do whatever he wanted. This obviously did not happen with the girlfriend. Stuart wrongly assumed that he could live thousands of miles away and do as he pleased with her remaining faithful because she could never do better. His ideas were rooted in pretensions, not reality. Fantasy allowed him to be a magnet, drawing to him sexually desirable females and males. This perception of himself as unique and irresistible, and therefore not bound by laws or mores that apply to others, was a critical error in his thinking. The culmination of its expression, along with other thinking errors, resulted in the brutal rape.

INDECENT EXPOSURE

I received a call from Mark, who told me that his career and perhaps his life were over. Mark was facing criminal prosecution after being arrested at a park by plainclothes detectives who had filmed him exposing himself. "I'm not sure anything can be done," he said, his voice shaking. Mark was so despondent that he had considered driving his car off a cliff. Understandably, his initial worry was the legal situation. It turned out that, fortunately, his chief concern was how he could be sure that he would never do anything like this again.

If there were ever a crime that seemed out of character, this was it. With the exception of one speeding ticket, Mark had never run afoul of the police, and had never been arrested. A highly educated man with a doctorate, he had quickly risen to a very high level job and held a top secret security clearance. He was slated for promotion to a position in which he would have major influence in determining the direction of an agency's policies. The prospects for that happening now or ever were nil. His marriage, already frayed, was unraveling. He said that the only reason he did not commit suicide was that he was "too chicken to do it."

When Mark and I met, despite his embarrassment about being "a flasher," he already had resolved that he would hide nothing. "I've had this problem my whole life," he confessed. His earliest memory was exposing himself at the age of seven to a group of relatives. Mark's parents admonished him, but dismissed the behavior as childish immaturity. No one could have imagined that this incident was the harbinger of a pattern of behavior that would persist for decades. During one phase of adolescence, he exposed himself on an almost daily basis. After nearly getting caught, he dropped down to once a month. In college, it occurred every couple of months. Before he was arrested, Mark exposed himself "every day that I had time," which meant on any day when he could leave whatever he was doing. During our first meeting, Mark was eager to talk about other personal problems and denounced himself as a "smug, conceited, arrogant son of a bitch."

Mark grew up regarding himself as uniquely qualified at whatever he undertook. Exceptionally smart and very determined, Mark seldom encountered failure. His commanding personality and a keenly analytic mind propelled him rapidly up the career ladder. The power that he wielded in his job and the admiration of his colleagues inflated an already titanic ego. People considered it a privilege to be granted a few hours of his time for consultation. He expected others to yield to his superior knowledge, and for the most part, they did. Considering himself almost incapable of error, Mark was incredibly intolerant and impatient with others' shortcomings. If people didn't do things in the particular manner he deemed acceptable, he was angry and critical. He recalled nearly mowing down a man who momentarily had blocked the road while clearing snow from a driveway.

Mark knew lots of people but had few friends. He treated his wife like a child and was unceasingly critical of both her and his daughter. "I attempt to manage the whole damn house," he observed. He nitpicked over the most trivial details with an attitude that no one could take care of things as well as he. If dishes were not stacked in the dishwasher in a particular manner, Mark would dress down the culprit. His wife characterized him as "a demanding perfectionist." She said that if dinner were five minutes late, he would react as though the world was coming to an end. Watching the evening news with him was an ordeal, as Mark would yell at the television set, cursing the action of public officials or whoever else was the subject of the report. Whatever anyone else said or did, Mark knew better!

In reality, Mark was not so perfect. Although he insisted on dictating everything related to family finances, Mark was outspending his salary, piling up debt, then borrowing money. His irritability and impatience resulted in his wife and daughter walking on eggshells, reluctant to differ with him. They were so put off by his moodiness that they often ignored or avoided him. There were times that Mark was miserable to be around because he just didn't want to bother with other people. On such occasions, he remembered treating his daughter in the same arbitrary and offhand manner with which he treated the annoying pet spaniel. Mark's irritability and reclusiveness often worsened when he had gone for a long period without exposing himself. Mark was relieved when his wife and daughter went somewhere together, for it gave him more time for exhibitionism without having to account for his whereabouts. Otherwise, if he went out alone, he'd have to have a plausible explanation for where he had been.

As the weekend approached, Mark's mind raced with anticipation as he thought about exposing himself. On Saturday mornings, the desire was so intense upon awakening that he had to force himself to undertake whatever commitments he had for the day. The urgency of these thoughts would be so immediate that, as soon as he could get out of the house, he went "hunting," as he called it, searching out opportunities to expose himself at parks, bike paths, running tracks, and other recreational facilities. (While speaking with me, Mark came to the realization that he never enjoyed the outdoors "like a normal person.") As he hunted, he paid attention to whether the person was male or female, young or old. He tried to figure out where they were going and what they were up to. His thinking was the same whenever he walked his dog, ran errands, or went jogging. An hour's errand could easily stretch into several. Mark reached a point where thinking about exhibitionism had such a priority that it not only determined his schedule for the weekend, but he also regularly worked it into his weekday schedule. As busy as Mark was, he found opportunities to take time away from work (e.g., an extended lunch hour) so that he could "hunt" and expose himself. Hunting required far more time than the act itself.

Indecent exposure consumed Mark's life to the point that he engaged in hunting even when he traveled on business. Prospects for indecent exposure were better out of town than at home because anonymity was more assured. Mark especially liked locations visited by tourists, such as boardwalks and beaches. In a strange town, no one (including the police) would know him, and he would be unlikely to return to the place he selected. Mark commented that just as people allocate time to play golf, he would build into his schedule a half day to case out places to expose himself. He'd select hotels to stay in not by their cost, particular features, or closeness to the work site, but by the opportunity available for exhibitionism. Because he exposed himself from hotel windows, the location of the room was important. If he were up too high, he couldn't be seen. If he were on the first floor, he could be identified more readily. Thinking about indecent exposure was so automatic that while attending a conference, his mind would drift to gazing out windows to scan the surrounding area for a place to expose himself. He recalled experiencing a "rush" at a professional meeting when he glanced out a window and spotted two girls running on a wooded path adjacent to the conference facility.

With great excitement, Mark anticipated the response when he displayed his penis. Although he told me that any kind of response was gratifying, his aim was to attract women, who would stare and find him irresistible. He'd be disappointed when a woman expressed shock and disgust, then instantly left. Mark did not regard his victims as victims. To him, they were barely human. He said, "I didn't think of them as people. They were objects. They were part of the game. I looked for young, attractive people."

From the time he started thinking about the "hunt," there was excitement. Describing the scouting out of different areas, Mark said, "My blood would be pumping." The excitement mounted as he found a location and strategically positioned himself. He commented, "The longer the whole thing went on, the better it was." He became physically aroused and, no matter what the female's response was, he masturbated after she left. Whatever Mark undertook, he expected to succeed, indecent exposure being no exception. Mark recalled that when he was much younger, he took greater precautions not to get caught. For example, he was careful always to wear different clothes for each occasion, never any with distinctive markings. As he got older, he became more confident that he could outfox the police. He told me that he was absolutely convinced "I was too smart to get caught." And by any standard, he was successful during all these years. He had even exposed himself more than a dozen times at the very park where he finally was arrested.

While discussing indecent exposure, Mark made no attempt to justify or rationalize his conduct. Nothing that he said supported explanations that are frequently offered to explain exhibitionism. He asserted that this behavior had nothing to do with sexual deprivation, because he engaged in it even after having sex with his wife. Nor was it to seek relief from any adversity or dissatisfaction. He had no recollection of exposing himself because of depression, and Mark noted that he didn't do it when he was under unusual stress. He asserted that the only accurate explanation is that "I crave excitement, and I enjoyed doing it."

Mark emphasized that "this rewarding recreational activity" was not a compulsion over which he lacked control. Exhibitionism was a planned activity, the result of a series of decisions. He reflected that even when he exposed himself to relatives as a young boy, he knew right from wrong. Finding exhibitionism to be "pure exhilaration," he emphasized that each time he made a deliberate *decision* to seek that excitement. He constantly assessed the risks and refrained when the odds of success seemed unfavorable. Mark called indecent exposure "a low risk, high consequence offense." He was more active in warm weather than when it was cold. He reflected that he could not remember a positive association with the advent of spring. Whereas characteristically people think about budding plants, flowers, and outside projects, he associated nice weather with a better "hunting" season. Thick foliage allowed for more places to hide. Mark compared himself to an animal stalking food. In the winter, he did it less but looked forward to spring. In calculating how much of his life he had spent at "this time consuming hobby," he estimated there were thousands of thoughts and innumerable incidents that likely would be equivalent to 15 24-hour days a year for nearly three decades. Mark acknowledged that fantasies about rape were also among the steady stream of thoughts flowing through his mind. We have no way of knowing, had he not been arrested for indecent exposure, whether Mark might eventually have acted on these fantasies.

. . . .

Stuart and Mark were at different stages of life. As a young adult, Stuart was establishing an identity in terms of educational and career plans and interpersonal relationships. Mark was set in his life's work and had a family. Interestingly, neither had close friends, although they had admirers. Despite one having a girlfriend and the other being married, neither man had intimate relationships. Scathingly critical of his wife, Mark rarely showed her respect, much less affection. He treated his daughter like a pet that could be amusing or a nuisance, depending on his mood. Neither Mark nor Stuart derived sexual satisfaction from a loving relationship.

Both men were accustomed to achieving success at whatever they set their minds to. Having received commendation for high quality work,

Mark and Stuart approached new ventures with supreme confidence, certain they were uniquely qualified for any undertaking. Real life achievements were gratifying but did not come close to offering the high voltage excitement that they derived from fantasies about their sexual irresistibility.

For Mark, the thrill was in the hunt as he located stations where he tried to entice passersby with a display of his penis. For Stuart, nothing matched the excitement he experienced while conjuring up sexually sadistic scenarios in which males as well as females would be drawn to him and gratify his every wish. Originating and orchestrating the sexual acts through his writings allowed endless possibilities. When these lost their power to arouse, Stuart revved up the excitement through his own form of hunting. Had the police detected Stuart stalking women and masturbating in public places in his car, he would have been arrested long before his most serious crime. Stalking had been another "success" in that he was too clever to get caught. His life as a free man ended once he became emboldened enough to transform years of rape fantasies into an actual attack.

No error in thinking by itself accounts for a crime. Many thinking errors in combination give rise to irresponsible or criminal conduct. The perception of the self as irresistible plays a key role in the behavior of rapists and sexual exhibitionists. These offenders are not likely to declare outright that they are irresistible to others. This perception of the self became evident rather quickly in my interviews with Stuart and Mark. It clued me in to their personalities. Recall Stuart describing his rape victim not as a victim but as "somebody who'd fall in love with me somehow." Recall Mark telling me how he figured that he'd stop women in their tracks and lure them by exposing himself. Neither man even alluded to the impact of his conduct on others.

A sense of uniqueness also plays a role in these crimes. Of course, everyone is unique physically and psychologically. The thinking error lies in considering oneself so unique that what applies to others, including certain laws, does not apply to oneself. People like Stuart and Mark pay lip service to what they share in common with others, but a pervasive sense that they are singular, one of a kind, separates them from the rest of the world. They are a law unto themselves and see no reason to be accountable to anyone else.

Stuart and Mark had such a mindset. I could hear it as they talked about the people in their environment. When Stuart dropped out of college, he turned a deaf ear to his parents' reasonable suggestions that he seek professional help and take a break from school rather than drop out altogether. Confident that he knew what course was most prudent, Stuart had not the slightest intention of spilling his guts to a counselor. His mind was made up, and he did not want anyone attempting to dissuade him. Stuart and Mark lacked friends because they had contempt for others and considered themselves far superior. They were adept at going through the motions and playing the game of appearing sociable, collegial, or whatever else a situation might require. When it came down to it, their interest in other people extended mainly to how they could use them for their own purposes.

In addition to the thinking errors of uniqueness and irresistibility, other thinking errors played a role in the criminal behavior of Stuart and Mark, including:

- Trying to control others;
- A failure to put oneself in the place of other people;
- Unrealistic expectations.

NOTES

1. "Fatal Addiction, Ted Bundy's Final Interview," edited transcript on the Internet from Dobson, James, *Life on the Edge: Pornography* (Nashville: Word Publishing, 1995).

CHAPTER 11

"I Think; Therefore It Is"

THE DETHRONING OF A "QUEEN"

I received a call from a locally well-known criminal defense attorney who intrigued me as he talked about a case he wanted to refer for evaluation prior to trial. Mary, a retired social worker in her fifties, had been arrested for possession of nearly $1 million worth of drugs that police had found in her suburban home. The attorney said that, in his experience, this offense was "highly unusual for a woman of her background and experience." Mary had never been arrested for anything in her life.

While legal proceedings dragged on, I had four months to get to know Mary. From the outset, she emphasized that she had been raised as "a Southern belle from a very fine family" whose lineage she had traced back to colonial days. Mary declared that using illegal drugs was something she'd never considered, even during adolescence. She said she had nothing in common with people who inhabited the sleazy world of drug users and dealers. They were not part of her social circle. "I hardly know people who drink," she sniffed. When I asked how she became involved with drugs, she replied, "That's why I'm here. It simply doesn't fit," by which she meant it was out of character.

It is against the personality I thought I had. I can't believe I did it. It's like it's this other person. I was cultured, poised, elegant, had a good personality. I'd be comfortable walking into the White House without any etiquette coaching.

Mary had married a man who was a hardworking government administrator. She complained that after he retired, he quickly began deteriorating physically and mentally to a point that he was "crazy wild—like Jekyll and Hyde." She said that he offered no companionship, and she was afraid she'd end up taking care of him and depleting their finances so that she'd end up on the street. At one point, Mary asked for a divorce, only to be told by her husband that he'd be dead soon enough and she'd have all their assets, which he assured her would be more than sufficient for her needs.

This lady reminded me of a man who said about committing burglaries, "When I walk into a room, everything in that room belonged to me." The burglar was not delusional. He knew he had entered someone else's residence. He realized that, in a literal sense, the contents of that home belonged to its owner. However, as he surveyed the living room, everything in it was his. He merely had to figure out how to take possession of it. Mary's thinking was similar. She was entitled to whatever she wanted.

Mary said that fear of being destitute in her old age drove her behavior. Terrified by her husband's disintegration, she became resolute that she would never suffer the same fate. Consequently, she devoted more and more time to her appearance, pampering herself, dressing "more exquisitely, wearing beautiful jewelry which I had rarely worn because my friends couldn't afford it." She thought about applying for another job but didn't think she'd be compensated sufficiently for the hours she'd have to put in. Mary explained that her dalliance with drugs occurred because someone sympathetic to her situation offered a way to make money quickly. "It was like I lost my values," she sighed.

That explanation, although possibly true, seemed awfully facile. Was it really the case that a woman of impeccable honesty (and a social worker) became a drug dealer? If so, then what Mary did was definitely out of character and represented, as she called it, a complete "moral disintegration."

During the many interviews that we had, Mary did her utmost to convince me that she was a singularly talented person who "inspired jealousy or admiration" on the part of family, friends, colleagues at work, and even the most casual acquaintances. Mary asserted that even her mother was jealous "because she wasn't as well put together as I was." Even as an infant, Mary was unlike other babies. She told me several times that she did not take nourishment from a baby bottle but imbibed "from antique cordial glasses" given to her by an elderly uncle. Mary said with pride: "We were the kind of people they call beautiful people. Everywhere we went, we were popular. I was treated very special—the brightest, the most talented."

Mary declared that she was more popular than her sisters, but she was also more of a risk taker, an excitement seeker, the family rebel. "I was always into trouble," she said mentioning an attraction to guys on motorbikes and engaging in other behavior that, she commented, "in my family was thought unseemly." No matter how appalled her family was by her conduct, she recalls always being treated "as if I was the queen." On the one hand, Mary spoke of her distinguished family pedigree. On the other, she described her parents and other family members as being crazy, mentally ill, and not particularly accomplished. After lauding her father's honorable character and citing her family's noble lineage, she complained that her family never did anything for her. Whatever the truth, she believed that she was to the manor born. And so she lived large, despite her county social worker's salary. What she earned bore little relationship to what she spent. The person who supported her lavish lifestyle was her husband Paul, whom she constantly denigrated. At 4 A.M., he arose in order to earn additional money at a part time job before spending a full day at his regular government job.

Paul told me that his wife demanded a huge, but unaffordable, house. She complained that she was embarrassed to entertain friends in the home they had. She had no more space for her antiques, her close to 200 pairs of shoes, and so many clothes that she could not stuff any more into the closets. The house was so jammed with her purchases that she remarked, "When we meet in the hallway, we have to go sideways." When Mary found what she called "the world's perfect house," she assumed she and Paul would be moving into it. Paul's absolute refusal to encumber them with a large mortgage infuriated Mary. Her insistence on making this move did not square with Mary's desire to ensure stability and comfort in her old age. But this is how Mary thought. If she wanted something, she should have it. In her mind, she already was thinking about what colors she'd paint the walls and how she'd arrange the furniture. The financial reality was something she chose not to think about. Mary regarded herself as the one with the brains, the vision, the shrewd judgment, and the good taste. Paul was an incompetent, bumbling idiot who, she complained, was "constantly looking for fights." The reality is that Paul was endeavoring to rein her in and keep them solvent.

Mary complained that Paul did not know how to enjoy life. Never did she concede that she had anything to do with this. Quite the contrary, for she declared, "I was his rock, and he's lost his rock." Thinking this made it so. Mary asserted, "I have nursed this man and propped him up all these years." Paul had a very different point of view. He became worn down and finally concluded that fighting Mary was taking too large a toll on his health and their marriage. Eventually, they began living separate lives. "She had freedom to do as she wanted," he informed me.

Although Paul had his flaws, Mary found him deficient no matter what he did. If he expressed interest in where she went, who she saw, and her activities, he'd be accused of being controlling and oppressive. In fact, Mary said about Paul, "He treated me like a slave—do this, do that." Once he adopted a live-and-let-live approach, she accused him of not caring and refusing to communicate. The partner who chose not to communicate, of course, was Mary. Paul commented that nearly every day she'd disappear without explanation, that he saw less of her than when she was working at her full time job.

Paul no longer had a partner in marriage, but an adversary. Mary considered household chores unworthy of her time. He did the grocery shopping and cooking because she regarded both a waste of her time. Whatever Paul liked, Mary had contempt for. She said that her husband wanted a "prefab place in the boonies," then commented, "I'm not a boonies person." As to his taste in furniture, she commented, "I don't have early American bric-a-brac. I have good things." Mary reported that they shared so little in common that they did not eat the same food. "He liked simple country cooking," she said with disdain, then noted, "I was a gourmet cook." If his wife's claim was true, Paul saw no evidence of it, for he told me, "She can burn water." Mary called Paul a cheapskate and complained about his pinching pennies by driving an old car and having them remain in the "same small house."

The question was, how did Mary spend her time now that she was retired? Where was she going and with whom? If she was a gourmet cook, as she claimed, for whom was she cooking? One thing was obvious. She spared no expense on her wardrobe and physical appearance. She spent close to $2,000 for cosmetic dental work and was contemplating cosmetic surgery for her nose.

While vilifying her husband, Mary expressed certainty that Paul was involved with another women, an allegation he denied vehemently. Paul told me that there always seemed to be men in Mary's life, but "I didn't push it." He had long learned that pressing his wife for information or explanation about anything led only to bitter arguments. He commented, "Since we were married, I'd ask her about a lot of things she did, and she'd say, 'I don't want to talk about it.'" Paul concluded that it was best to keep the peace, because confrontation was unpleasant and futile in terms of getting the truth.

Mary thought she was still a hot commodity, for she told me:

Any man I view as a prospect is younger than I am. I didn't go through this middle-aged thing of feeling I'm undesirable. I've had constant offers. I'm comfortable with men. I have no problem...I have a high IQ. I had it all—my fine family and background. Men tell me they were honored to be out with me.

Mary confessed that she had developed a relationship with a "love-friend," an "upper-class gentleman who had attended a ritzy school." He was married, more than a decade younger than she, and very wealthy.

You might think Mary was simply a blowhard and a braggart. But she truly believed that she had it all in terms of admirable personal qualities and that she therefore was entitled to whatever she wanted. When she told me that she thought that by selling drugs, she could salvage a tolerable life for herself in her old age, that rationale did not hold water, for it was inconsistent with other disclosures. She never saved proceeds from drug sales for a future nest egg. Instead, she spent wildly on "frivolous things."

To live the glamorous life that she thought was her inherent right required considerably more income than she and her husband, two retired government employees, were receiving. When Paul married Mary, he rescued her from credit card debt by paying her long overdue bills.

She took for granted his bailing her out and continued her voracious shopping. Paul commented, "She has no concept of value." As an example, he mentioned that when he was out of town, Mary paid an outrageous sum to a man for routine yard work, then doled out more cash as an advance toward future work. If Mary wanted something, she'd make the purchase on the spot. Price was seldom a consideration. Paul said that his wife could wear a different dress every day for two months and never repeat an outfit. Paul referred to his spouse as "Imelda," after the wife of the Philippine president who was notorious for owning hundreds of pairs of shoes. When Mary tired of clothes, she donated them but never bothered to obtain receipts for charitable deductions.

Paul believed that Mary's involvement in drug sales had nothing to do with providing for her old age. He informed me, "We had more money coming in than I needed. There was sufficient income for her to live well." They both had retirement income from pensions, income from investments, and they owned a home that had appreciated substantially. Paul stopped pressing his wife to account for what she spent, although he surmised she had started giving money away to friends who would adore her for her generosity, then owe her favors in the future. Mary never stopped thinking about money she wanted to spend on herself, even when she got out of prison: "I'll need a face lift, body lift, and spirit lift."

Being extremely private, Mary seldom took people into her confidence. While employed as a social worker, she minimized interactions with work colleagues. She had no interest in them, because she felt she shared nothing in common. Mary expressed contempt for her entire profession, asserting that she entered social work as "the chicken's way out," by which she meant that she considered it an easy path to take because it offered the security of a regular paycheck and fringe benefits of sick and annual leave.

I didn't want to be a [social worker] to start with. I'm a natural at at a lot of things. The first time I picked up a violin, I could play it. I'm good at anything I'm interested in. There's not enough hours in the day to do all I'm good at...I can see a dance and do it instantly.

Mary was so abrasive with co-workers that she nearly got fired. However, she had a knack for sensing how far to push while managing to ingratiate herself with upper management. Mary bragged about how successfully she maneuvered at work so that she received "only the highest evaluations." She said, "There wasn't anybody I didn't know. I was in with the big boys. I didn't go through the chain of command."

Mary's angry personality eventually surfaced. The demure, genteel southern belle turned out to have rough edges. I had asked Mary about some of her husband's statements that he had made during several interviews. She was so upset by what her husband had related that she snapped, "I am absolutely irate; I feel violent." After her first meeting with the court-assigned probation officer, she was furious because that official told her she was "borderline rude." Paul and the probation officer were the two people who dethroned the "queen." These were quite possibly the only two people who refused to be snowed by her and who would not affirm the view she had of herself.

Mary's arrogance had no bounds. She was angry at her husband for portraying her as an "avaricious bitch." She smoldered with resentment toward the probation officer, whom she said had subjected her not to an interview but an "interrogation." Things must have gone quite badly, because Mary told me that the interview was "horrendous" and that she had been told she had an "attitudinal problem." Not one to regret anything she had said, Mary nonetheless knew she had failed to impress the probation officer, the very person who ultimately would prepare a report that a judge would consult before pronouncing final sentence. When the probation officer ordered her to attend drug counseling, Mary took it as "harassment." The drug treatment center staff could make no headway with her. A clinician's report to the probation officer stated that Mary refused to discuss information "that was even remotely related to the events of her arrest." The evaluation turned up no evidence that Mary had abused any illicit drugs. Thus, no treatment plan could be formulated.

. . . . .

Mary's responses to my questions contained all the thinking errors discussed so far—pretentiousness, uniqueness, and irresistability. During the first interview, the first thing she did after informing me of the charges against her was to mention her "long family lineage." Most clients seeking professional help do not begin by announcing their pedigree. Anxious, depressed, or whatever their problem is, they seek relief from distress and are not intent upon impressing the therapist. In contrast,

Mary's objective was to convert me to her point of view and minimize the consequences of the crime she had committed.

As she articulated her inflated view of herself, her *pretensions* spilled forth. Everything about her was the finest, the best, the most. She regarded herself as a highly gifted, multi-talented woman. This was her self-evaluation, which she believed others shared. She was eloquent in her self-presentation, but short on facts. All I knew for sure was that as a self-described "jewelry junky," Mary was good at designing jewelry. Her husband confirmed this talent when he told me, "She can weld and solder and make any kind of handcrafted jewelry." In fact, she had melted down some of her mother's silver in order to fashion jewelry more to her taste. And so she had chests of jewelry, much of it handmade. She sneered at the police thinking she used money from drug sales for jewelry.

That she considered herself *irresistible* was obvious as she spoke of her appeal to men, especially those younger than she. Mary also boasted endlessly about the caliber of friends who were drawn to her. While she touted them to be "individualists" and "straight as arrows," her husband remarked, "She picked up friends who seemed strange."

That Mary perceived herself as *unique*, one of a kind, was evident in her attitude that she was superior to other people in every respect. At the final meeting with me, which occurred shortly before her sentencing, Mary still was emphasizing her personal magnetism. She said not without pride, "I have a lot of male friends. All these people are saying goodbye to me." She commented that she even had two phone calls from men "who offered to get rid of my husband."

People like Mary have little need to question or evaluate their thinking. Feedback from other people is not welcome and is shut out unless it confirms opinions they already hold.

The thought process of "I think; therefore it is" should not be confused with a psychotic disorder, in which a person is psychologically impaired in differentiating between fantasy and reality. Mary held basic premises about who she was and what she was therefore entitled to. When these thoughts collided with reality, she characteristically blamed other people for treating her unfairly. Most frequently, she faulted the people with whom she associated most closely and on a daily basis, namely her husband or work colleagues. Seldom did it occur to her that she played a major role in creating circumstances that led to her own unhappiness.

From previous setbacks, she had learned virtually nothing. When Mary experienced a wound to her inflated self-image, she responded by branding people who thwarted her as ignorant, insensitive, disagreeable, or uncultured.

In depicting her husband as having a deteriorating Jekyll-Hyde personality, Mary was not playing for sympathy. She believed what she said based on Paul not behaving in line with her expectations. When Paul reached the limits of his endurance and started questioning his wife's spendthrift ways and other habits, their relationship quickly soured. Mary knew that the financial resources that she and her husband had were not without limits. She realized that Paul was working harder than anyone she knew. Limits never sat well with Mary.

Mary was not just putting on airs. She appeared to believe everything she said. It would not enter her mind to economize as many retired couples do. Self-denial was totally alien to her way of thinking. In fact, Mary's appetite for expensive material possessions increased the more time she had on her hands. By selling drugs, she gained the opportunity to acquire quickly far more money than she could ever earn by re-entering the work force. In retirement, she could continue her reign as the regal southern belle.

I never knew for sure whether Mary had crossed the line into illegal activities in the past. Once she established herself with a drug supplier and customers, she knew that what she was doing was illegal, but it was right for her at the time. And because she believed this, it was so!

Perhaps no one was more stunned by Mary's arrest than Paul, the person who supposedly knew her best. As Paul returned from having dinner with friends and approached their home at night, he saw a number of cars in the driveway. His first thought was that Mary was having a party. He was dismayed to discover that the "visitors" were police officers. When he learned that a million dollars worth of drugs along with scales for weighing out the portions had been seized, Paul was shocked. He told me that his wife didn't even smoke cigarettes, much less use illegal drugs. All he heard from Mary was that her objective was "to create a sum of money with the thought of leaving me." That she wanted to leave was news, because Paul thought they had worked out a way to coexist relatively peacefully.

Mary did not level with me about the details of the crime. She did say that she had been methodically pilfering money, a little at a time, from the account she and her husband still had together. She had accumulated enough to start buying drugs. She told me that she was caught because a customer got arrested, then cooperated with the police. Mary said that the police believed that she had been a drug dealer for a long time. She huffily denied this to me. She was indignant as she accused the police of doing what she did all the time—leaping to a conclusion, then proceeding on the basis of what they thought. The difference was that the police had marshaled incontrovertible evidence!

A different path that a mental health evaluator might take would be to focus on Mary's family, her upbringing, and early development in order to figure out how she had become the person she is today. I devoted time to taking a history, but this process was of little value. Mary was not an honest person. She related so many different stories about her parents, siblings, and other relatives that it was impossible to separate fact from fiction. The "fine family" from which she came was not so fine after all, for eventually, Mary disclosed a family history of alcoholism, suicide, psychiatric hospitalization, and just plain weird behavior. It was impossible to figure out what was true. Paul told me that his wife refused to "volunteer any information about her family." An excursion into the past turned into a waste of time. Even if I knew I had accurate information, what help would it be to the court in determining what to do with this defendant?

To the extent that the *person* is considered, rather than just the nature of the offense, a judge or jury wants to know who the defendant is, how he or she has functioned in life. The judge would know Mary only as a name and as charged with a particular offense. My job was to make her human, to tell the court about her personality, her character, the good and the bad. What happens to a defendant while growing up, if it was truly traumatic and could be verified, might be offered as a mitigating factor in some courts, possibly reducing the severity of the sentence. There is usually far more interest in how a defendant dealt with whatever his or her life circumstances were rather than in the circumstances themselves. In this case, relevant factors were: how Mary had coped with the challenges life has handed her; how she had utilized opportunities to develop her abilities and talents; what was important to her; how she had dealt with frustration and disappointment; how she had gone about making decisions; to what extent she had learned from past mistakes; whether she thought about potential consequence to herself and others; whether Mary took responsibility for the current offense; and, finally, whether she was remorseful.

In my evaluation of Mary, the only time she showed that she had a softer side, something different from being the imperious queen, was when she admitted feeling badly about what she had done to Paul: "He's pretty nearly had a nervous breakdown. The guilt is upon me. He doesn't deserve anything like this. I really, really feel guilty about this."

I am not saying that Mary's specific crime, her involvement in the murky world of drug sales, was predictable. Certainly the secrecy, the intrigue, and excitement involved in making large sums of money quickly and easily suited Mary's character. The riches that she knew would be hers would enable her to enhance an already lavish lifestyle. She was accustomed to success and to having others defer to her. Had she succeeded in her enterprise as a drug distributor, Mary's already grandiose view of herself as unique and irresistible would have received quite a boost!

Needless to say, my report to Mary's attorney could not help her in court. It was never filed with the court, nor did I testify. However, my findings did help Mary's lawyer better understand his client and therefore assisted him in his preparation for trial.

CHAPTER 12

The Unimportance of Feelings

*T*hroughout this book, I have been focusing on thought processes, seemingly to the exclusion of considering the offender's emotional life. Like any human being, defendants in criminal cases experience a wide range of emotions, including depression, anger, excitement, stress, embarrassment, and so forth. In my forensic evaluations, I find that focusing on feelings contributes little to my understanding of the offender's character. *Emotions are generated by thoughts.* When a person speaks about being depressed, it is important for me to know what thoughts are producing this emotional state. Is the person sad because he is having thoughts about a personal failure? Is he thinking about a deceased friend? Is he depressed because his girlfriend walked out? What thoughts prolong or relieve the depression?

I remember a depressed middle-aged lady (not a defendant in a criminal case) whom I counseled when I first opened my practice. She said little except that she was sad and didn't know why. I learned from her husband that she constantly feared disappointing people. He said that she was a wonderful person but regarded herself as a failure because she was not the perfect wife, perfect mother, perfect housekeeper, perfect caretaker of her own mother, and perfect employee. Having this much information, I discussed with this lady the expectations she had of herself. As she slowly realized how unrealistic she was, she changed her thinking. The depressive feelings subsided, and she became more energized and productive.

I can select any criminal case file, open to the notes that I took during interviews, and locate statements in which the defendant gave considerable emphasis to his or her emotions. While writing this paragraph, I did just that, grabbing a file of notes taken during my evaluation of Loretta, an accomplished professional woman who was arrested for shoplifting at a department store. Having no prior criminal record, she described her illegal conduct as "not my character, personality, or values." Loretta's references to her feelings included:

- "I felt alone."
- "I was like in a daze."
- "I felt it was like a veil coming down over my face."
- "I worried too much."
- "I felt I had to work harder and harder. It gives you a lot of angry feelings."
- "My depression went harder as time went on."

These statements indicate that Loretta experienced loneliness, confusion, anxiety, and despair.

Sometimes people use the words "feel" and "think" interchangeably. If I ask how you feel about what you are reading, I am asking, "What do you think?" If I ask how you feel about a candidate running for office, I am inquiring into your opinion—what do you think about him? If you are especially enthusiastic or negative, you may respond with intensity (i.e., emotion) to the question.

Because I interview people in circumstances that they find distressing, they frequently complain about being depressed. I remember my first meeting with Grant, a man awaiting trial on a charge of first degree murder. When we first met, Grant stared at the floor, responded to questions tersely in short sentences, and spoke in a monotone. He stated that he was depressed, but didn't elaborate. I had no idea whether he was depressed about himself, about something that had transpired just before he met with me, about his legal status, about what occurred during a phone conversation, or about the food in the jail. Did Grant's depression call for psychological or medical intervention? Was he suicidal? A videotape would show an obviously unhappy inmate, but it would reveal nothing about what was going on in Grant's mind.

When I asked Grant to explain what he was depressed about, his demeanor changed. He perked up and, with considerable animation, told me he was upset that he was rotting in jail instead of being treated at a psychiatric facility where he thought he belonged. He was frustrated by his lack of success at convincing the authorities that he should be transferred to a hospital. Why did he think that a hospital was the most appropriate place? I asked. Sensing that he now had a forum in which to make his case, Grant unleashed a tirade asserting that he was confused at the time he killed a young woman who was his friend, that he still had no idea why he did it, and then declared that he shouldn't be punished for being mentally ill. He emphasized that if he were to receive treatment, he would recover and be able to live in the community rather than be compelled to waste his life in prison. Grant was depressed about his circumstances, not about himself.

Grant's "depression" was different from that of Mark, the man who, after being arrested for indecent exposure, was contemplating suicide. The former was upset only about his circumstances. Mark was despondent as he anticipated a domino-like set of consequences—the loss of his security clearance, being fired from his job, his wife leaving him, losing the respect of colleagues, and the embarrassment from publicity surrounding his case. But, unlike Grant, Mark was also depressed about himself and informed me the first time I spoke with him that, whatever the legal consequences were, he knew he must get help to stop indecent exposure and to make other changes about the way he was living his life.

Let's return to Loretta and her statements about her feelings. I probed to reconstruct the thinking that generated the emotions she described. Exploring statements about loneliness, I learned that she brought it on herself. She was so uncompromising that she drove others away. Arrogant and impatient, she considered herself a superstar at whatever she undertook and had no tolerance for others' mistakes. Because she was intimidating and disagreeable, others steered clear of her. "I worried too much" was not a reference to a person overly concerned about other people. Rather, Loretta was consumed with worry because she had difficulty getting co-workers to like her and cooperate on the job. She fumed about having "to work harder and harder" because, as a nitpicking micromanager, she thought others were incompetent and therefore it was imperative that she do everything herself. In a moment of reflection about

her expectations, this prima donna said to me, "Nobody was supposed to make any mistakes." She acknowledged that her husband was constantly urging her to stop being so hard on people, to show more compassion, and give others a break.

Speaking about her feelings, Loretta said that while shoplifting she was "in a daze" and had the sense that "a veil came down over my face." When I inquired about her actual thoughts while in the department store, Loretta disclosed that, in truth, she was mentally lucid and supremely confident about what she was doing. She recalled, "I felt right at home, like the stuff was already mine." When I inquired if she intended to pay for the stolen items, she replied, "I didn't even think about it."

Loretta spoke about experiencing depression that worsened over time. Never did she seem depressed about any failure or personal shortcomings. As was the case with Grant, she was depressed about the sequence of consequences unfolding after her arrest.

Mental health professionals frequently emphasize helping clients "get in touch with their feelings" and express them. During forensic evaluations, I have found that if I were to focus on feelings, I would land in a bed of quicksand from which it would be hard to extricate myself. Offenders use their feelings to justify and explain anything and everything. They also tend to describe feelings as though they are external to themselves and not at all subject to their control. Some offenders go a step further and try to enlist a mental health professional to embark upon an archaeological expedition to delve into their personal histories and thereby discover the source or cause of their feelings. It is far more useful to ask the offender in detail about the thinking that gave rise to a particular emotion than it is to focus on the emotion itself. Getting lost in the briar patch of feelings is a time-draining diversion from assessment of the offender's character.

CHAPTER 13

The Defendant's Use of Language

*T*hus far, I have emphasized that understanding the world from the offender's point of view is at the heart of a psychological assessment. Conducting an evaluation requires an awareness of my own preconceptions and setting aside theories about what caused the particular behavior. Such an assessment requires at least temporarily disregarding diagnostic labels that may already have been assigned as explanatory but are likely to conceal more than they reveal. My focus is on developing an understanding of how the offender thinks, as though I had access to a computerized printout of his thoughts as they occur in his mind, without interpretation, rationalization, or explanation by him or by me. As indicated earlier, this is a formidable task when a person is being held accountable for a crime and faces serious consequences.

In cases discussed thus far, I have highlighted specific thinking errors, with additional errors to be discussed. This is as good a place as any to discuss how the offender's use of language often differs from common usage. I am not referring to street slang or to obscenities he may use. Rather, everyday words have a meaning in line with an offender's view of life. To avoid misinterpreting what offenders say, it is important to realize that the meaning they give to words arises from their worldview. The Larrys and Stuarts of this world not only think differently from people who are basically responsible, but their use of language reflects this difference. Understanding how a person uses even a single word can open up a new vista.

Let's return to Larry. A person who approaches adversity by attempting to avoid or destroy it differs from an individual who perceives adversity as a challenge and a problem to solve. Larry regarded his mother as offering both the road and the impediment to love, success, and money. Instead of establishing an independent life with his own career, Larry counted on his mother and manipulated her. While taking full advantage of her hard work in building a business and her personal generosity to him, he saw her as a formidable barrier to fulfilling his dreams. Constantly frustrated, he wished her out of his way, then finally killed her. The manner in which Larry used certain everyday words reflected his idiosyncratic world view.

Love is a word that I have seldom heard offenders use except to refer to sex or sentiment. The offender does not have loving relationships, if "loving" involves putting oneself in the place of another person, showing compassion, loyalty, appreciation, and trustworthiness. Larry professed to have loved his mother. He tearfully told the police officer after he killed her that there was no one in his life whom he loved more. She most likely found him to be a loving son as long as she gave him money or whatever else he wanted. Mark, who exposed himself to others, professed to love his young daughter. A videotape of his life would show him playing with her, fondly joking around, and bragging about her achievements. There was probably no one else in his life toward whom he had such deep sentiment. But on weekends, when he had opportunity to spend time with her, he spent hours searching out sites to expose himself. The lives of those whom Mark "loved" were shattered when he was arrested. This man was oblivious with respect to protecting those who cared most about him and who also depended on him.

The offender looks at people mainly in terms of what they will do *for* him or *to* him. A mother is not viewed as a human being. She is perceived primarily in terms of what she will give him. A parent is adored so long as the offender gets his way. This was certainly true with Larry. Even as a young adult, he didn't think of his mother as an individual with her own personality, her own desires, fears, and hopes. He assessed her value in terms of whether she contributed to or interfered with his achieving his objectives. He never cared about knowing her for the person that she truly was.

To *understand* something means to comprehend it. However, offenders frequently accuse others of failing understand them. Mary characterized her husband Paul as almost incapable of understanding her. Paul often questioned her about whom she was with, where she was going, and how she spent her time. Paul understood what she said; he just didn't approve. Mary would declare that a misunderstanding had occurred whenever anyone did not accept her explanations and rationalizations for her conduct. By claiming to be misunderstood, offenders like Mary shift the focus from their behavior. The effect is that the person accused of a misunderstanding may believe he is the one with the problem.

Any of us might think another person didn't understand something we said. However, we don't habitually accuse others of misunderstanding in order to cover up wrongdoing. For example, a high school senior asks his father to use the car on Friday night. The parent declines permission. The teenager grouses, "But Dad, you don't understand." His father comprehended the request perfectly. There was no "misunderstanding." He simply refused permission because another family member already had been promised the use of the vehicle. Offenders regularly dig themselves into holes, then take the spotlight off their misconduct by accusing others of failing to "understand."

Another assertion many offenders make is that they were not accorded the *respect* they were due. Their response to being "disrespected" may be lethal. We respect others for a personal trait such as kindness or for a particular accomplishment. We respect a national symbol such as the flag. We respect an authority such as a parent or teacher. This is very different from a man requiring that another person respect him just because he demands it. A motorist grows impatient with the seemingly deliberate pokey driving of the man in front of him. He signals and passes, only to have the other driver suddenly accelerate and scream obscenities. Road rage takes over, with the slower driver now furious that the other driver failed to respect him. A person with such a mentality expects to prevail in every situation. This has nothing to do with earning respect.

Each of the offenders whom I describe in this book is of at least average intelligence. Some, like Mark, are brilliant and extremely accomplished. Yet, they lack knowledge of basic concepts of responsible living that are second nature to most children before they reach adolescence. Ricardo, an offender whom I have not discussed previously, was a scholar of the classics and could quote Plato and Aristotle. He was a beloved teacher at a junior high school. For all his education and ability to engage students in learning, he still ended up serving time in a federal prison convicted of embezzlement. Ricardo considered himself to be highly trustworthy. He frequently lectured students on the importance of trust in relationships. A charming and sophisticated man, Ricardo had a series of girlfriends who came to depend on him. He insinuated himself into their lives, exploited them for money and sex, then discarded them like used napkins. He professed to love each one and considered himself trustworthy and deserving of their respect. *Love* and *respect* were demanded but not shown toward others. In Ricardo's thought processes, *love* and *respect* had very different meanings than they have to most people. From his perspective, if women loved and respected him, they'd succumb to his charms and give him the sex and money he wanted. In the lives of men and women like Ricardo, human relationships are perceived as avenues for conquest. Words take on idiosyncratic meanings depending on the offender's thought processes.

Paranoid is a word I have heard offenders use with some frequency. Henry, a defendant in a murder case, told me that he was paranoid about his supervisor at work. It turned out that Henry came to work late, composed personal e-mails during work hours, enjoyed extra long lunch breaks, and frequently missed deadlines. Paranoia is a condition in which a person is suspicious without a basis in fact. If I tell you that the state and local police are out to get me, that would be a paranoid delusion. The man with the disgruntled supervisor had every reason to suspect that his boss was on his case for his frequent violations of work rules and policies. Henry's suspiciousness, or what he termed his paranoia, arose from real events. Fed up with the liberties Henry was taking, the supervisor was watching him and documenting his infractions in writing. Henry was close to being fired.

Offenders frequently say they are *bored*—that "nothing was going on," that they had "nothing to do." Well-intentioned reformers advocate establishing recreational programs and other time occupiers as antidotes to boredom. It would be well worth the cost if more basketball courts, sports leagues, and social programs could ameliorate this boredom that offenders complain about. Give a criminal a chance to play basketball, and the result will be a criminal who plays basketball rather than one who doesn't.

The thought processes of the person do not change because he has a sport to play! In fact, an offender whom I interviewed told me how bored he was living in a small town. He complained that all there was to do was "just play sports." To relieve boredom, he took off for the city, which was 30 miles away. In search of "action," he quickly figured out where to go. Becoming involved in a gang, he eventually was arrested for attempted murder.

We all know what boredom is. A long car trip on an unscenic, congested interstate highway can be excruciatingly boring. A lecturer may drone on in a boring monotone, lulling his listeners to sleep. Many of us occasionally experience tedium in day-to-day living, then lapse into fantasies of lazing on a beach or flying down a ski slope. The criminal may have similar experiences. But his complaints of boredom characteristically refer to a lack of excitement, a dearth of what he considers high-voltage activity. When he says he has nothing to do, this is light years away from many of us, who lament that in an entire lifetime there is not sufficient time to do all that we want. "Nothing to do" for a criminal means nothing satisfies his incessant craving for excitement. You may remonstrate, "What's wrong with excitement?" There needs to be more to life than working, paying bills, cleaning the house, and carrying out other routine chores. A responsible person's desire for excitement may be fulfilled in many ways, but it does not require building himself up at the expense of others or engaging in illegal activities. By endeavoring to understand life from the offender's point of view, we avoid the mistake of assuming that he and we are attributing the same meaning to commonly used words or expressions.

When men and women like Mark, Stuart, Mary, and Anna acknowledge they have made a *mistake*, we should not jump to the conclusion that they are owning up to error. When Fred was finally caught for embezzling funds from a public agency, he expressed regret. However, his regret was not for betraying his employer. Mainly, he lamented his carelessness that led to his apprehension. He had gotten away with what he had done for so long that he grew cocky. A mounting sense of invincibility had resulted in sloppiness that triggered an internal investigation of what turned out to be a glaring accounting error. The "mistake" was in lowering his guard. One man whom I evaluated characterized a vicious assault that he had committed as a mistake. This in no way indicated that he felt remorseful about his brutality. Rather, it was an expression of regret about not spotting a witness who was able to identify him to the police.

If you were to discuss ideas of *right and wrong* with any of the offenders whom I have mentioned, you would find a consensus. They knew their offenses were illegal before they committed them. They also could readily engage in an earnest conversation about what constitutes moral conduct. In the strongest terms, Anna and Larry would have condemned the killing of another human being. Mary had contempt for anyone who used or trafficked in illegal drugs. All knew the potential consequences or what I would term the occupational hazards of crime—getting caught, convicted, or confined, and possibly getting injured or killed in a high risk crime. However, upon deciding to commit a particular crime, the act, as they saw it, was not wrong. Criminals have a remarkable capacity to eliminate considerations of right and wrong long enough to commit a crime. What they want to do at any particular time is "right." Clearly, any worthwhile discussion of right and wrong requires that we understand this way of thinking.

Each of the men and women discussed so far were extremely lonely, despite having people who cared deeply for them. Mary acknowledged how alone she felt in her marriage, how isolated she had become from work colleagues, how deserted she felt as friends pulled away. Remember Steven, the young man who abducted his girl friend's uncle? He had a close-knit family who loved him and took pride in his achievements. While attending college, he had professors who took him under their wing. Colleagues at the lab where he worked nurtured the career of this promising young scientist. Yet, Steven had no close friends and was a very lonely man. Detached and aloof, he was obsessed with what that lay beyond his grasp—total control of his girlfriend, who pulled away the more she felt smothered by him.

When a criminal speaks of being lonely, usually it does not refer to a lack of companionship or of caring people. He imposes loneliness on himself. Secretive, not inclined to trust, he is an island unto himself. He takes far more than he gives. Mark's wife and daughter adored him. In contrast, he paid lip service to but did not truly reciprocate their affection and caring. His wife's role was to serve him by running the household and arranging life at home to suit his convenience. Mark seldom participated in routine aspects of child care such as feeding, bathing and changing his daughter when she was an infant. As she grew older, Mark showed little interest in her day-to-day school work, activities, or friends. He took pride in his daughter's excellent grades because they were gratifying to his ego. It is difficult to imagine such a highly educated, accomplished man leaving his family and even his job to find locations to position himself and exhibit his penis to unsuspecting passersby. Mark appeared to be a family man. The reality was that, upon awakening on a Saturday morning, his thoughts immediately turned not to his family but to how to get out of the house as soon as possible for his solitary hunt.

Everyone has private aspects of his life that he does not disclose. The criminal is lonely because he chooses to be a loner. He is intent on concealing his desires and plans because he knows that even those who care most about him would disapprove. He experiences less loneliness when he engages in something he considers exciting. When Anna was on the computer consumed by "cybersex," she had no sense of loneliness. The same was true of Stuart while he was stalking young women. He experienced a gnawing letdown and loneliness after he trailed a female to her home, sat in his car fantasizing and masturbating, then drove home to explain to his worried father where he had been so late on a school night.

When I first began interviewing offenders, I'd be pretty sure I understood what they were telling me. Then I'd be thrown a curve ball in which I'd be accused of misunderstanding what was said. A man would speak of his paranoia. I thought I knew what he meant, for I had studied the condition. However, I was puzzled, because I heard no evidence of delusional thinking. A man would complain that he had been bored, and I thought he just needed more to do. Meaning would seem to evaporate from these conversations. The offender might as well have been speaking one language and I another for all the communication that was occurring. But I thought I understood!

CHAPTER 14

Having a Thin Skin: Susceptibility to Putdowns

*A*lthough criminals have an image of themselves as indomitable, unusually clever or slick, and always in control, they also are supersensitive. Think of it this way. If day in and day out you expect everyone to function on your terms even in the most minute aspects of life, consider the intense and frequent frustration you would experience when something went wrong. You start your day expecting breakfast on the table when you want it, a smooth commute, a problem-free day at work, a quick commute home, a gourmet dinner on the table, and peace and quiet while you relax the rest of the evening. The reality is that a day without frustration or disappointment is rare. "Murphy's Law" states that if anything can go wrong, it will. We are well acquainted with Murphy in that not a day passes without some irritant, if not a significant impediment to our plans. Sometimes we deal with Murphy well, other times we could do better. For the criminal, Murphy does not exist. From the time he arises until the time he sleeps, his chess-board view of life prevails. Like pawns on a chessboard, people are to behave as he expects.

When anything happens contrary to the criminal's expectations and demands, he takes it extremely personally. He regards as a "putdown" whatever fails to support his image of himself as a powerful person. Being told what to do is a putdown. Having to ask a question of another person is a putdown because it shows him to be less than omniscient. Having someone disagree is a putdown. Although he freely dishes out criticism, he takes it poorly, responding as though his entire self-worth is being attacked. If he elicits criticism by his own misconduct, he blames others. If his wife is irate because he failed to call and arrived home three hours after dinner was ready, it's her fault. She shouldn't be so demanding. If his girlfriend exchanges a few words in conversation with a male acquaintance whom she encounters in a store, he is quick to conclude she is flirting and takes offense.

A putdown exists only in a person's mind. If we are criticized, we can consider whether we deserve it, then possibly benefit. If we think we don't merit the criticism, we can disregard it. The criminal thinks in all or nothing terms. Any tiny detail of life that doesn't go his way can result in a catastrophic response, almost like the rapid deflation of a balloon when it is pricked by a pin. This is because he perceives his entire self-image as being at stake. When an offender saves a seat in a public place for his buddy, that chair already belongs to him. He is ready to go to war if someone else occupies it. Furious because he has been deprived of what he regards as belonging to him, he engages in an angry exchange of words or an assault. In the last chapter, I discussed the criminal feeling put down and retaliating when he does not get the "respect" he demands. Being "disrespected" is a severe putdown. People have paid with their lives when offenders retaliated in response to what they interpreted as a putdown!

No matter how many hundreds of offenders I interview, I keep in mind how hypersensitive they are. Still, I occasionally am surprised by their dramatic reactions to what seem to be innocuous topics of conversation. I had counseled Morris for more than a year while he was on probation. As April 15 approached, I asked this 35-year-old man whether he was pre-paring a tax return. He blandly remarked that he was certain his mother had taken care of it. Having spent the last several years in jail, Morris had earned no income, and so taxes were not on his mind. I pointed out that recently he had worked several months at a restaurant and that he might need to file a return. (He might even be eligible for a refund if taxes were withheld.) When Morris replied that he didn't know how much he had earned, I suggested he call his employer and obtain a statement of his wages. I mentioned that a public official recently in the news might go to jail for failing to file income tax returns. To my surprise, Morris, normally mild-mannered and eager to please, exploded and shouted, "Fuck all this!" When I asked why he was angry, Morris made it clear that he had felt put down, for he retorted, "I don't like appearing ignorant." Fortunately, Morris wanted to change his ways, and we were able to discuss the income tax subject further. He looked into the matter, phoning his employer and obtaining a statement of wages and tax withholding.

"A LIFETIME OF INSULTS" RESULTING IN A HOMICIDE

Wally stabbed his wife to death in the kitchen with a butcher knife as they quarreled over a financial document. The homicide occurred while a custody battle was raging over the couple's five year old son, Kenny. I was asked by the defense attorney to evaluate Wally's state of mind at the time of the crime. This crime was a shocker, for it was committed by a man who appeared to be a stable, solid citizen. A father and architect, Wally had no criminal record. He never used illegal drugs, seldom drank wine or beer, and the only blemish on his driving record was a speeding ticket. Wally described himself as "easygoing, very helpful, and reasonable." How was it that this "reasonable" and accomplished person committed what appeared to be an irrational and lethal act?

A logical place to begin my questioning of Wally was to ask about the custody issue. Wally and Diane were married 12 years before they separated. Wally commented that he hadn't known Diane all that well when they married. It wasn't long before conflicts arose on every front, including money, in-laws, and housekeeping. Wally said that his wife used sex as "her power issue," bestowing it when she thought he was worthy of her favors. He remarked that his wife was so attractive and seductive that "everyone would fall in love with her." Wanting a family and afraid to be alone, Wally stayed in the marriage long after he suspected Diane of having an affair.

Wally said that he and his wife engaged in "nasty, vicious word battles." He became infuriated as she picked at everything from the amount of money that he earned to weight that he was gaining: "Nothing I could do would please her. She could whip up my anger and passions in a matter of seconds. I thought I deserved better. . . I felt I was doing all the giving. She was doing all the taking." During the first half hour of our initial meeting, Wally remarked, "I buy into negative things people say and do not recognize the good things." He said he felt increasingly vulnerable to Diane's attacks. He would let what she said get under his skin and dwell on it. Consequently, he lived in a near-constant state of feeling put down, deflated by her criticism. Wally alleged that Diane bombarded him nonstop with comments about his shortcomings.

The truth was that Diane had reasons to be dissatisfied. Neglecting his health, Wally had become extremely obese. He had been less than successful at work, getting fired and bouncing around to different positions.

Wally maintained that Diane could not get to him on any issue like she did with regard to custody of Kenny. After the marital separation, Wally concentrated on the fierce custody battle. Maintaining that his relationship with Kenny was "super close," Wally asserted that he and his son were "best buddies." He told me that he had gone "on a crusade" to prove that he was the better parent and the child's primary care provider.

Being a father meant everything! Wally asserted, "The one thing I've really succeeded at is being a father." Although he and Diane had joint custody of the child, Wally was shattered when, through the assistance of a private investigator, he discovered that his worst fear had come true. Diane had a boyfriend, and there was a possibility that she and her paramour might move out of state and petition the court to take Kenny with them. Wally told me, "I didn't want to be a visitor in my son's life. I was at their mercy. I knew Kenny would go with his mother."

Wally said that he watched his wife gradually and perniciously turn his son against him, comparing her manipulations to a dictator rewriting history. Not only did he fear that Diane would succeed in alienating Kenny, but he also believed that the court would favor a child of Kenny's age being with his mother. "I know it's not popular for fathers to get custody of small children," he told me. As Wally saw it, their joint custody agreement was meaningless, for he remarked, "She was not committed to the agreement. This was my Achilles' heel. I was being jerked around too much."

Wally had lost his wife. His health was failing. He expected to be fired any day from his job. Kenny was all he had left, and that boy meant the world to him.

That boy's my life. I even wanted to die for him....Kenny was my safety valve. He'd come and crawl on my lap, and it'd all go away. It didn't matter what the bitch was doing. I felt better with Kenny. I worried about him when I wasn't with him.

Being a super father was all that Wally had left supporting his self-esteem. He said that his self-confidence was higher when he was with Kenny then at any other time.

People with whom I spoke thought Wally was far too focused on Kenny, that it wasn't healthy. A neighbor who knew Wally, Diane, and Kenny commented: "He was obsessed with Kenny. This kid was everything. He was emotionally tied to Kenny. The custody matter was like life or death. He'd smother the kid." A close friend of the couple had observed the dynamics between Wally and Diane. He witnessed Wally going into a tailspin over Kenny's custody, that it "remained an obsession....that's all he had to live for." The friend further noted, "He competed with [Diane] for Kenny's affection. They were both expert in yanking each other's chain. They'd stake out positions. He had a temper. A lot of vinegar and bile would come out." Diane knew her husband's weaknesses and precisely how to goad him. Wally recalled that while they lived together, "She'd try to pick fights with me in front of Kenny just to get me going."

Long before the separation occurred, violence was no stranger to this marital relationship. Wally recalled numerous times thinking about hitting his wife. He deterred these thoughts because he was certain "she'd run to the police and say I brutalized her." At times, husband and wife grew so enraged they'd pick up the nearest object and hurl it. Wally recalled that, during an especially violent argument, Diane screamed that she wanted to kill him. He recalled wishing that he "could have belted her." Instead of physically lashing out, Wally started beating the wall, pounding the pillow, and hitting the mattress.

Wally not only thought repeatedly about assaulting or killing Diane, but he also contemplated killing himself, figuring that suicide was "the best, the most logical thing." He couldn't bring himself to do it because he was "too chicken," and he also feared he might fail (as he had at so much else) and end up grossly disabled. Furthermore, Wally believed that Kenny would suffer enormously without him as his dad.

On what turned out to be Diane's last day of existence, Wally recalled having reached a point where he couldn't take any more. Certain he would lose his son, he concluded that he had been defeated by "the bureaucracy and judicial system." Deciding he at least could get closure on several unresolved financial issues, he arranged to meet his wife at her home to have her sign several documents. That did not go smoothly: "She signed and bitched about how I was cheating her. I wanted her to stop beating on me. I got pissed off, really angry. Why was I even bothering?"

As the subject turned to Kenny, Diane declared that she could take him any time, anywhere, and boasted that she would win in court. That turned out to be the final straw —the ultimate putdown—in what Wally called "a lifetime of insults."

It was as though the obvious had been revealed—that she had this crystal clear plan, that she had duped me, that the fears I had—that she dismissed—were real. All that sort of welled up....It was her planning to take Kenny away and leave the area, and I wouldn't see him anymore.

Wally recalled "getting madder than hell." A struggle started in one room, then they proceeded into the kitchen, where he grabbed a knife and stabbed her. It did not take police long to track down Wally and arrest him. He was sentenced to nearly four decades in prison for first degree murder.

Through my interviews with Wally and collateral sources, it became evident that Wally felt put down in every aspect of his life. His entire opinion of himself as a good and worthwhile person had collapsed!

Wally assumed little responsibility for anything that had gone wrong, and he had lost perspective as to what had gone right. He had had problems at work and was positive he was about to lose his job. The reality was that his employer knew he was going through a rough time during the custody litigation and figured Wally's performance would improve once the matter was resolved. He had no intention of firing him. Wally did lose Diane. However, there was little likelihood that he would lose his son, because Diane had no plans to leave the area because of her career, friends, and family.

In speaking with others, I heard about additional instances in which Wally exploded in response to a perceived putdown. A court evaluator told me that Wally had catastrophic reactions to his wife's provocation, turning "mean and vindictive." A family friend said that Wally was quick to take offense and "fly off the handle." And a close relative observed, "His life was on a rubber band. It went so far, and then it snapped."

. . . .

During the past 23 years, I have been involved as an independent evaluator in hundreds of cases in which there has been bitter litigation over child custody and visitation. I have seen men and women who loved each other become mortal enemies, then ruthlessly pursue custody of a child as though it were a trophy and a referendum on their own self-worth. During the custody litigation, they try to inflict emotional and financial wounds on each other, but they do not physically annihilate their "enemy."

Wally's homicide was not an out of character crime. He was a man who responded to adversity not by taking it as a challenge to cope with, but by taking it as a personal affront! Many times in his thinking, he had gotten rid of Diane. When he finally killed her, it was in response to the one putdown too many.

The term "putdown" is not used by criminals. It is a word that is descriptive of a mental process that occurs habitually in the inner life of the individual. If an offender is counting on something to happen, it is a sure bet. Thinking makes it so. Anything that stands in his way constitutes a putdown—a threat to his ego.

Wally had an exceedingly thin skin. He dished out criticism and lashed out in anger but refused to take it from others. He was chronically angry at a world that, from his standpoint, treated him unfairly. His anger was perpetually simmering within, often not observable to others. Like a cancer, it metastasized and then erupted in a lethal manner. Diane's boast that she would win in court turned out to be the one thing too much. She paid for those words with her life.

Some people who are not criminals are hypersensitive. They take criticism poorly even if it is offered in a constructive fashion. In such instances, criticism taps into self-doubt that the person already has, what have been called "feelings of inferiority." Wally did not think he was inferior to anyone. In fact, he thought that he was unique—a parent without flaws.

During my evaluation, Wally revealed many errors in thinking. He regarded himself as the only suitable parent for Kenny. (There was no evidence that Diane was a bad parent.) He demanded that others affirm that view, especially the court. Among other thinking errors were the following:

- A failure to deal with adversity in a constructive manner, instead fantasizing about and then killing the person whom he saw as the source of his problems;
- Assuming without facts that the court would rule against him;
- Blaming other people for difficulties that he created or contributed to himself;
- Failure to adopt a long-range view of the situation, which would include his mounting a persuasive court case rather than taking matters into his own hands.

The most serious thinking error was his becoming so blinded by anger that he failed to put himself in the place of his five-year-old son, who wanted only to love and be loved by both parents. Kenny became an orphan—his mother dead, his father in prison. Wally's comment toward the end of the evaluation revealed that, months later, he was thinking not about his son but about himself, for he commented, "The wrong parent got killed is what it all boils down to." From Wally's standpoint, one parent or the other had to die. There was no room in this world and in Kenny's life for both parents to exist.

ARMED ROBBERY

When 19-year-old Bill's mother learned about his holding up a convenience store, she could not believe it. She told me, "I was absolutely devastated. It was like the floor opened up and I'd been swallowed." Other than a schoolyard fight, Bill had no history of violent behavior. His father commented, "Bill's a good kid; I've never known him to hurt anybody." Bill was employed, was enrolled in a class at night, and had a girlfriend whom his parents liked very much. As an adolescent, he had been a Boy Scout, nearly attaining the Eagle rank. He aspired to become a veterinarian.

A defense attorney asked that I evaluate Bill, hoping that I would be able to assist at the sentencing hearing. The crime was calculated, planned several days in advance. Bill held up an establishment where he had previously worked. He was familiar with the premises, including the security measures, and he knew precisely what time of night the manager opened the register and prepared the bank deposit. He committed the crime wearing a ski mask so that no former co-worker would recognize him. He had the brazenness to return the next day to the scene of the crime and, with a new shift on duty, innocently say he had heard about the robbery, then inquire whether anyone had been hurt.

I met with Bill at the jail, a place he had never dreamed he would see the inside of. Frightened and very somber, it appeared that he had decided to come clean and speak candidly with me. He seemed to be saying that what he did was out of character, for he said, "That wasn't me who robbed the place." When I asked what he meant, Bill replied, "It was a different me. I have two different personalities." There was the good kid who tried to please others. Then there was the boy who was on the wild side. During eighth grade, Bill's parents separated, and he had far less supervision, a situation which he welcomed. Both his mom and dad felt guilty about the divorce and felt he had suffered enough because of them. Consequently, they took a sort of hands-off approach. Bill lived with his mother, who was less restrictive than his dad. He commented about his mom, "She just tried to please me. I took advantage." Since both his mom and dad worked at full-time jobs, there was no one to supervise him from school dismissal at 3 P.M. until 7 P.M. Bill started hanging out with older kids and skipping classes, occasionally missing entire days. At the time, the school was lax about reporting truancy, and so neither of his parents was informed.

Beneath Bill's polite veneer was a boy intent on permitting no one to get in his way, no one to "mess with" him. Small slights loomed as major putdowns. Bill reflected, "I could get angry so easily." He remembered an incident when he entered a store to use the bathroom. Because the line was long, he went outside to urinate. Apparently, a boy who saw him made a disparaging remark "about my private." Bill instantly became infuriated: "I punched him and slammed his head against the wall and kicked the crap out of him. That was in the days when I was very violent." Although this was not his only fight, Bill volunteered that it was "the first fight where I ever made anyone bleed." His father, who did not think of his son as a violent person, commented that Bill could be moody. He remembered one occasion when Bill flew into a rage at his brother and smashed a window.

Bill said that when he drank alcoholic beverages, "anything could get me upset." Then he would be super sensitive to putdowns and more likely to respond physically to conflict. He'd react to advice or help from his parents as a personal affront. Arguments with girl-friends over seemingly inconsequential matters flared into major altercations.

After readily owning up to truancy, drinking, defiance of his parents, and several assaults, Bill's demeanor quickly changed. Tersely, he said, "You make it sound like I'm a piss poor kid, like I was a piece of shit." Angry and tearful, he said, "Maybe I wasn't that good, but I always meant to be good." Bill dissolved into tears and became angry. He protested that I was wrong about him, then shut down, shrugged and said with muted hostility, "Whatever!" He explained that he desired only "to make other people happy." In a matter-of-fact manner, I asked how he expected his mom and dad to be happy when they disapproved of his behavior. That question did not help the situation, and again Bill felt put down and replied, "Whatever!"

I realized that Bill felt put down. In focusing upon bad behavior, he thought I was ignoring what was good about him. Bill's anger subsided both because of his desire to make a good impression and because I verbalized that I understood what he was upset about. The young man then acknowledged, "I get upset easily," and volunteered that I had given him a lot to consider.

I'm trying not to face it. You're making me face it. I have to grow up. I can't live the imaginary life I think I'm living... I didn't think I hurt my parents, but I probably did. It's kind of shocking.

In Chapter 8, I discussed the offender viewing himself as a good person. Thinking seriously about the harm he has done is extremely unpleasant. Being portrayed as a victimizer is out of line with the offender's image of himself as a good person. The fear of a putdown is so pervasive in the offender's personality that anyone who deals with him traverses a minefield. A particular word, an inflection of the voice, or a look has the potential to trigger an explosion.

ARSON

After Carl had been arrested for setting several fires, he was referred to me by his attorney for a psychological evaluation. His parents were very much in favor of the assessment, because they were totally stunned and baffled by their son's behavior. Setting a fire was the last thing they could imagine him doing. They knew if Carl were to be convicted, he would have no possibility of entering the career he had talked about since he was a little boy. A volunteer at the local fire station while in high school, Carl could hardly wait to become a salaried fire fighter. He had taken hundreds of hours of hands-on training classes, equipping himself to become an emergency medical technician. Carl had no criminal record and was not known as a troublemaker in his rural community. His mother declared that what her son was charged with was so "out of character" that she found it impossible to believe he could possibly be guilty. Yet, Carl had confessed to the police that he was the arsonist.

Carl was at a loss when it came to explaining his conduct. He seemed reticent and emotionally bland, yet surprisingly confident that his parents, lawyer, and I would bail him out of this jam. He was like a person standing outside and watching a drenching storm approach, but remaining confident he'd stay dry. To understand Carl's behavior, I explored topics that at first seemed far removed from the crime. A family member had related that Carl would change in a flash from being self-composed and caring into a bully who smashed property, including his own belongings. His sister likened Carl's sudden transformation to turning a switch on and off. When I asked Carl about this, he acknowledged becoming infuriated so quickly that he could not recall what set him off. I concluded from speaking with family members that Carl was hypersensitive, that he perceived putdowns in a disapproving look, a disparaging word, and even in a mild reprimand by parents, teachers, or others.

Carl was moody and difficult. Not adept at dealing with the give and take that relationships require, he attracted few friends. Seldom did he endear himself to teachers. In the rare instances when Carl liked a subject, he applied himself and performed extremely well. Mainly, he despised his teachers, neglected assignments, and absorbed little of what was taught. Carl did so poorly that he twice had to attend summer school in order to get promoted to the next grade.

I have emphasized in this book how vital it is to find out, then explore, what is most important not to the interviewer, but to the offender. With Carl, there was no mystery as to what his passion was. As I asked about his life as a volunteer fire fighter, Carl grew interested, animated, and outspoken. He voiced a longing to be important and gain recognition and expressed intense disappointment and anger when he thought he was being thwarted. Carl and I discussed the culture of the fire house, at least how he experienced it. His relatively small station was often passed over for fire calls in favor of other stations that were larger and better equipped. All stations within the county had an intense rivalry with one another. When Carl heard other volunteer fire fighters at his school disparage his station, he took it extremely personally. Whereas other fire fighters took the jokes, digs, and occasionally nasty comments in stride, Carl found them intolerable and stewed over them. He recalled fretting over several of these comments shortly before he set one of the fires. Carl remarked about the fires he set: "I wanted to show we could get the job done. I took it hard [i.e, the insults]. I know about fire house pride. It hurt!"

Carl indicated that he had conflicts with fellow fire fighters at his own station. He seethed when he thought his ideas were disregarded. He was furious when someone else received recognition for a suggestion similar to what he offered. He couldn't endure being ignored by those who "played favorites." Carl bristled with resentment whenever a younger volunteer "got bossy" and tried to exercise authority over him.

When Carl set the fires, he knew that, as a volunteer, he would see action. No more sitting around being bored; he'd get to "run a call." What mattered was the excitement of all that would transpire once the fire was reported. Carl would hear the call come in, then be among the first responders physically present on the scene. Putting his training to use, he could be a hero.

. . . .

Men and women who have a psychological makeup similar to Wally, Bill, and Carl respond angrily to anything that happens in life which fails to confirm their inflated image of themselves. The Wallys, Bills, and Carls of this world expect others to accommodate them, rather than vice versa. They are constantly disappointed by people who do not respond as they expect. For Carl and the other offenders whom I have described in this book, anger was constantly present, even if not directly observable. When, like a cancer, the anger spread, anyone or anything could be a target. In a personality like Carl's, one putdown too many can result in a cataclysmic event. One young man whom I evaluated was embroiled in conflict with his parents for years. Many times in his thinking he had gotten rid of both of them. On a day when his mother insisted that he check himself into residential drug treatment, he exploded and stabbed her to death. Her demand was the last putdown he'd endure!

CHAPTER 15

The Self as the Center of the Universe

*C*riminals seek to preserve an image of themselves as powerful and unique individuals. They care little about the emotions, opinions, dreams, or aspirations of other human beings. Were they to be genuinely interested in other people and demonstrate empathy, they would encounter a great deal that fails to support their exalted opinions of themselves. As I have indicated, these people do not announce their intentions to others. Most seem like anyone else, desiring to have a family and a well-paying job and wanting love and respect from others. However, these individuals are not willing to subordinate what they want to making sacrifices that family life requires. They desire well-paying jobs but may be unwilling to work hard. Attaining legitimate positions of power and prestige does not satisfy them. Demanding love and respect, they are unwilling to do what it takes to merit them. Thinking solely of their self-interest, they consider any means to an end as acceptable. Criminals live as though the world is a giant chessboard, with people being the pawns for them to move about at their whim.

A "LOVER" OF BOYS

You will now meet Mike, whom others considered a sensitive man because he appeared to demonstrate unusual empathy. In the decades that I have spent evaluating offenders, I found Mike to be one of the most self-centered individuals I have encountered. He believed that his sexual activity with young boys was not a victimization at all, but that it contributed to their well-being.

Mike was convicted of sodomy and taking "indecent liberties" with children. He was arrested after neighbors complained to the police about frequently hearing noisy kids in the hallway and wondering about all the children entering and leaving Mike's apartment. Mike's defense attorney asked me to conduct a psychological evaluation prior to sentencing. Describing himself as "extremely law-abiding," Mike had no criminal record. A college graduate and a computer programmer, Mike received outstanding job performance evaluations. He had never used illegal drugs and drank alcoholic beverages seldom and only in very small amounts. His driving record was perfect. Known as an extremely high-caliber guy, Mike was the last person people would suspect of doing anything unseemly.

Mike described his arrest as "a tremendous trauma." I would find it characteristic that, through more than a dozen interviews, this man would remain focused on the trauma he experienced while declaring repeatedly that he hurt no one. Instead of being remorseful, Mike reveled in recalling his sexual contacts with countless young boys, his preference being children between ten and thirteen who were just reaching puberty. He said that if he could relive his life, he would have "done a lot more." He made statements such as, "Our relationship was wonderful" and "It was like being on cloud nine." Mike was emphatic that he had total control of his sexual impulses, even pointing out that he chose to refrain from sexual contact with minors during several years when he did not want to jeopardize a job that required a security clearance. During that period, his sex life was restricted to pornography and his own fantasies.

This man was unapologetic about having sex with boys. He seemed to celebrate it and relished going into details of sexual acts occurring at his apartment furnished with a king-size bed, mirrors, and "romantic" lighting. He explained that he truly cared about kids, that he wasn't one of those creepy men who hide in bushes and lure children into sexual activity. He encountered boys at swimming pools, malls, and playgrounds. Once Mike befriended a boy, he was introduced to the youngster's friends. He emphasized that he built relationships with kids, helping them cope with conflicts at home, assisting them with school work, and relating to them in ways that boosted their self-esteem. Mike said that he responded to their curiosity and questions about sex by educating them with magazines and pornographic films.

Mike commented that, despite what people might think, it was not true that he was "nice to them to get into their pants." Mike pointed out that boys are attracted to him, that if they had been uncomfortable with what was happening, they would not have kept returning. He said that sex occurred spontaneously as it might in any close and increasingly intimate relationship. Mike observed, "Most boys, once you've developed a relationship, are very interested in sex." He contended that some of the boys initiated sexual activity, even insisted upon it. Mike emphasized that he never resorted to intimidation or force. Asserting, "None of these boys thought of me as a child molester," Mike said he would entertain thoughts of killing anyone who might molest a boy with whom he had an emotional connection. He described his relationships with boys as nurturing, comparing them to bonds between fathers and their sons: "I like kids; I love to be with them. I love to help them. I'm like a surrogate father in a sense...I am one of the few adults they can talk with. That's sad. They can't talk with their parents."

As Mike discussed these relationships, it became apparent that nearly all the boys came from very troubled families. On occasion, he got to know a parent. He mentioned helping one boy's mother in her struggle to abstain from alcohol. He dated the mother of another. Ingratiating himself to a parent gave him almost unfettered access to the child.

Patiently, Mike explained, "Your way of looking at it is so different. It's hard to find a common ground." Interviewing this defendant was not difficult, because he was eager to answer any question. His overall objective was to educate me, in fact to convert me to his point of view that sex with children is a good thing if you love them, not evil as many uninformed people think. Mike emphasized the natural spontaneity of engaging in sexual activity when men and boys love each other. Speaking about himself and others who share his sexual proclivity, Mike commented:

Boy lovers we prefer to call ourselves....Any pedophile I have met adores children. It's almost like a religion....Once boys know and like you, the sexual flows out of it. It's not like you're setting them up. There's no trap! Young males are interested in young males their own age but, given a chance, they prefer an older male, which I don't understand. They won't volunteer this, but once they confide in you, this comes out.

Mike contended that not only was he giving pleasure to boys eager to receive it, but he was also teaching them something useful: "The boys don't consider it homosexual. They learn how to make love, and it's transferable. What we have done, they do with their wives and girl-friends."

Mike acknowledged that sex with boys was on his mind constantly. He said that the best antidote to depression was just to see a boy. He'd get an intense "adrenaline rush" by watching boys undress in locker rooms at swimming pools.

I asked Mike if he worried about legal consequences. He replied that since he was a child, he was aware of the illegality of having sex with young children. He explained that he agrees with the intent of laws that protect children from being molested. He asserted that his situation was totally different, and nothing was inherently wrong in what he was doing. "They can tell me I broke the law, not who I love and don't love," he declared. Indignantly, Mike said, "They call me a molester when these boys were thriving. I'd be in less trouble if I had beat them up." Mike discovered that some boys did not know that the sexual activity was illegal, so he would warn them, "It's against the law, and you could get me or yourself into a lot of trouble." He explained that, because these kids craved attention and sex, "they took great pains not to get me into trouble."

I asked Mike if these boys experienced an aftermath of guilt, knowing that their sexual activity with him would be considered abhorrent by their parents and by many others in society. He immediately dismissed this possibility, replying, "There's no trace of guilt. We just sit down and talk about it. Then they put it out of their minds." I asked whether he regarded the sexual activity as a betrayal of a parent's trust to befriend a boy, then have sex with him. Mike then made his only concession, "I agree. Most parents would not send their kids over to discuss sex or have a relationship."

As to whether a ten- or eleven-year-old has the judgment or maturity to make an informed decision about whether to have sex with him, Mike scoffed. He retorted, "This does not require decision-making; it's spontaneous." Asked why he did not restrict his relationship to being a good friend and helping a child, Mike replied, "It would take away a dimension." He said that "the sexual thing made the bond stronger," then added that the relationship was more important than the sex. He remarked, "Sex you hope for, but it you don't get it, that's OK."

It was evident that as a boy sexually matured, Mike lost interest. However, he asserted that the end of a sexual relationship did not necessarily terminate what had become a "friendship."

Throughout our interviews, Mike maintained he was a victim, not a victimizer. It was the "system," laws, and law enforcement that created the problems. He deplored "outside meddling," referring to parents who are "wrong in not condoning sex with their 13-year-olds." Mike pointed out that his "European outlook" is less judgmental than American Puritanism, noting that some countries do not outlaw consensual sex between adults and children. Mike said that in some cultures adults instruct very young children how to make love. He insisted that the boys benefited from their relationships with him; no harm was done. However, he was vehement in asserting that they were victimized and suffered greatly at the hands of police interrogators, social workers, and narrow-minded, ignorant parents.

Mike said that, although he was devastated by his arrest and the prospect of incarceration, his greatest deprivation would be the lack of contact with boys. "I've been punished almost beyond endurance not seeing them," he morosely told me. Mike was deeply saddened by accusations that he had harmed children who had placed "so much confidence and trust in me." Toward the end of our meetings and after his attorney put him "through the wringer," Mike claimed to finally understand something he had not seriously considered:

I can see better his point of view and thereby your point of view. I try to put myself in the place of a parent. It wasn't my place to do it [i.e., have sex with a child], not without permission.

He allowed that perhaps he might have abstained if he had focused on the unfortunate consequences that the boys would be subjected to once their relationship with him was exposed. Mike was horrified by the prospect of the boys being dragged into court and forced to testify. He considered agreeing to a plea bargain to spare both himself and the boys from having to endure a trial. Again, he assured me, "I really do like these kids, not just to get into their pants." He expressed the hope that, after the legal proceedings concluded, "they can forget about it."

Throughout my evaluation, Mike persisted in trying to get me to understand and adopt his point of view. He was emphatic that he did nothing wrong except break a law that an enlightened society should not have on the books, much less enforce. He maintained, "I'm not criminally inclined." He declared over and over that the last thing he wanted was to hurt any living being, especially boys whom he loved. He declared, "Where there is love, there can be no damage done." He said that in his relationships with boys, he exerted no power over them. In fact, he argued, if anyone had the power, it was the boy. Unwilling to consider seriously any view other than his own, Mike had given little thought to possible undesirable outcomes of his sexual contact with minors. It became clear that the following considerations never entered his mind:

- If befriending and helping a boy were his sole objectives, sex need not have been part of what transpired between them.
- By having sexual contact, Mike betrayed the parents' trust in him and in their own sons.
- Because children ages ten to thirteen are inexperienced and immature, they are vulnerable and easy to control. Thus, they can be prime targets for people like Mike. If they engage in sexual activity with a trusted adult, they are not likely to consider legal or other ramifications.
- Mike put the children in an untenable position when he instructed them not to tell anyone about what they were doing. Some must have found it confusing when , as their friend, he warned them they must keep secret the very conduct that he had encouraged them to engage in.
- Mike failed to consider the impact on a child when he discontinued the sexual activity because he no longer found the youngster desirable.
- Mike did not think about how his sexual involvement could affect the children psychologically, either at the time or in the future. He had no regard for possible adverse long-term effects the sexual relationship might have on the children's self-image and sexual development.
- Mike was not deterred by prospects of what a youngster might experience (embarrassment, stress during interviews by

strangers, the trauma of testifying at trial) if his parents and law enforcement officials became aware of the sexual activities.

As much as Mike professed to be a lover of boys, he was thinking primarily of his own needs. Although he may have helped some youngsters, the harm done likely outweighed any benefits. Hearing that one of the boys who had participated in the police investigation was furious with him, Mike was baffled and commented to me, "I can't understand it; it's a complete turnaround." Throughout the evaluation, Mike spoke only of his distress—being deprived of the companionship and love of boys, serving time in prison, having to start over again in his career.

You may think that Mike was not really a criminal, that he was a sensitive person who became a social pariah because of his sexual orientation. A great deal is unknown about the origins of erotic attraction. It is extremely unlikely that Mike would have freely chosen a life of being sexually attracted to young boys. His existence would have been easier if he were heterosexual. Nonetheless, Mike had choices to make every day in terms of how he would live. He could have functioned as he reported he had during four years when he limited his sexual life to fantasy and masturbation. He still could have enjoyed adult companionship. He had the skills to earn a comfortable living, and he had interests and hobbies to fill leisure time. However, to his way of thinking, life without boys was inconceivable.

Mike was so self-absorbed while pursuing what he desperately wanted that he ended up harming many boys whom he professed to love. Mike regarded his arrest and confinement as interruptions to the life he looked forward to living. He candidly told me that, eventually, he would move to a country that does not prosecute "boy lovers." He turned to me and said, "What's the harm?" He did not want a response.

A MASTER OF DECEIT

Tad was referred by his attorney for psychological evaluation after being charged with fraud against his employer. What he had done was to submit duplicate forms to receive reimbursement for business-related out of town trips. A weekly "road warrior," he was spending on each trip hundreds of dollars for plane fares, hotels, ground transportation, and meals. Tad benefited by $100,000 after a computer glitch resulted in depositing all reimbursements to each of two personal accounts. Tad knew that these funds were piling up in both accounts but took no steps to inform the proper people of the dual payment. A married man in his mid-thirties, Tad had no criminal record. His wife Joy received the shock of her life when a relative reported receiving a call informing her that Tad had been arrested. Joy thought the cousin was joking and failed to see the humor. Upon discovering this was no joke, Joy became distraught. She had had her problems with her husband, but she still thought of him as fundamentally honest, extremely hardworking, and faithful to her. She could not imagine that Tad had it within him to defraud anybody.

Complaining that no one believed in his innocence, Tad was determined to convince me that he had done nothing wrong. He attributed his legal dilemma to a misunderstanding rather than a criminal scheme. His employer overpaid him. He had no intention to deceive anyone. He said that he had been so preoccupied with the demands of his job that he neglected his finances. He acknowledged that, because he traveled so frequently, his life had become chaotic and he had had little time to attend to personal matters. Tad emphasized all he ever wanted was a good family life and success in his career. As it turned out, he had subverted both objectives. Acknowledging that he was "never a good organizer," Tad expressed contempt for "administrative stuff." He said that reconciling his checkbook with bank statements was "not on my list of priorities." Tad indicated that Joy was bogged down by being meticulous about trivial matters, then remarked that her being so "particular" was an expression of her controlling personality. It turned out that his disdain for being "particular" meant that he was willing to manipulate a situation and do what was most expedient to accomplish whatever objective he had in mind. Tad volunteered that while preparing his resume, he would "adjust the wording for each position" so as to give the best impression, noting, "I don't lie. I just leave things off." Tad acknowledged that he was so consumed by getting ahead that he had reached a point where he was spending little time with Joy, and it just became evident that she was feeling neglected.

Throughout this evaluation, Tad showed himself to be an angry, controlling person who insisted that others accommodate him. He even antagonized the probation officer assigned to his case, for he told me,

"She thinks I'm arrogant and cocky. She'll put me under the jail!" From his standpoint, the problem was that other people were quick to accuse and attribute the worst motives to him. He complained that others didn't see him as they should, that they failed to understand his good intentions. He acknowledged that he became hurt and angry when this happened (a statement of his vulnerability to put downs), and sometimes he blew up. Tad commented that if his wife had a complaint, she needed to figure out the right way to approach him.

Tad took it personally when people were late. He said it showed their lack of consideration and respect. Yet, he was chronically late, including for our appointments. This was a man who counted on others to tolerate any inconvenience he might cause them. Joy told me she dreaded traveling with him because of the stress generated by his last minute scrambling to get to the airport. As we discussed Tad's lack of punctuality, he commented, "It's a big adjustment to think of other people."

Many people procrastinate and fail to be punctual. Although this results in inconvenience to others, it does not mean that these individuals are criminals. With Tad, his general indifference to other people was the issue. In nearly every aspect of life, Tad was absorbed with Tad. People around him paid a price for his thoughtlessness. Because of his charm and affability, they were reluctant to criticize and allowed him a lot of latitude.

Joy's observations were important, because Tad had no objectivity about himself. Although Joy commented that her husband "doesn't have a grasp on responsibility and on his life," she remained incredulous that he would perpetrate a fraud on his employer, who had been so generous and offered him opportunities for advancement. Still protective, Joy commented, "He says he cares so much about other people that he doesn't care enough about his own life." Rather than view her husband as self-centered, Joy identified his major flaw as ignoring his own needs while overextending himself to help others. Joy thought that because Tad became "stressed out," he had temper outbursts. While emphasizing that her husband was a very good person, Joy did acknowledge that Tad could be "extremely aggressive."

I feel like a client a lot of times in our relationship. He wants things to go smoothly, not to have any problem. When I ask him to help me clean the apartment, he screams that I have an agenda.

During our interview, Joy let things drop about conduct of Tad's that she found distressing—"things that tend to not leave your mind." She volunteered, "Incident after incident over the years has opened my eyes. I don't think he deals with his emotions well."

Joy recalled a situation that occurred when she was driving with Tad in the car and another driver pulled into a vacant parking space. Even though Joy had no intention of taking that particular space, Tad jumped out of the car and screamed at the other driver. Joy said that her husband had pushed her and thrown things at her, although he never physically hit her.

Recently, Tad used Joy's car and received a 50 dollar parking ticket, which came in the mail in her name. After promising he'd pay for it, Joy received a notice that doubled the amount due because a late fee had been assessed. As we spoke, she still did not know whether he paid the ticket. And she dared not ask. Before this happened, Joy began thinking she couldn't trust her husband with money and opened a separate bank account.

Still wanting me to think well of Tad, Joy explained that her husband had "very low self-esteem" and was "always looking for praise and acceptance." As I questioned Joy further, she became less defensive of Tad and disclosed more. She was furious about his legal situation, because there seemed no end to the consequences. They had to spend thousands of dollars for a lawyer. They were paying for this evaluation. Looming over them was the likelihood that Tad would be required to make restitution of all the money that he had diverted into his account. From Joy's point of view, her husband had jeopardized everything they were working toward, and she could not fathom why. She pointed out that she worked, and that both of them were doing well financially. Everything that had transpired seemed so needless!

Joy finally acknowledged that she came to a realization that she had not known her husband well enough before they married, for they had dated just two months. Joy recalled her infatuation with Tad because he was "tall, handsome, charismatic, and charming." She said that she did not know his "true personality" and, before they married, never had the slightest indication of "his aggressive nature." Finding me a good person to whom to unburden herself, Joy said:

[Tad] thinks about himself, and that's it....I don't want to say he's violent, but there was a time when I feared him. Maybe it was partially my fault. He was mean and nasty to me. He held no consideration for others....He'll blame anybody but himself. He's quick to twist words and not take responsibility.

After obtaining Joy's permission, I spoke with Tad about what she said. He fumed at her portrayal of him. He snapped, "I'm not irresponsible," and attributed his anger to "being tired psychologically." He then returned to his main theme—that he was not to blame, that it was his employer "who wants to see me burned." Asked why his employer would have such animosity, Tad was at a loss, and replied, "That's what I can't figure out."

Tad's assertion that he was a "free spirit" meant that he considered himself free to do as he pleased, not to be encumbered by what he considered inconvenient and mundane details of life that were beneath him. Tad perceived himself to be like the hub of a wheel around which everything else revolved. If someone had an appointment to meet him, they might just have to wait. If his wife asked for assistance with a chore at home, she'd have to keep nagging and risk incurring his wrath. When I evaluated Tad, he was full of self-pity because he thought the world was against him. His employer wanted to "sink" him. The probation officer thought he had a "criminal mind" and wanted to incarcerate him. He was without a job and in debt by several hundred thousand dollars. From his perspective, none of this was his fault. Rather than recognize his own shortcomings, Tad continued to rail at a world that he found increasingly unsatisfactory. In the end, he pled guilty to a fraud charge and was placed on probation.

· · · ·

A major difficulty in interviewing defendants like Mike and Tad is that they are used to having their way. Apprehended for a crime, they still expect to prevail. Just because they face legal consequences does not eliminate their lifelong patterns of thought. Both men were referred to me by their attorneys. Unquestionably, they saw me as an ally. (I was evaluating them at the request of lawyers whom they had retained.) When they discovered that I was not so quick to take their statements at face value and believe what they wanted me to believe, they were dismayed.

People who commit crimes that appear to be out of character rarely have been held accountable for significant misconduct. They may have been questioned and doubted at times by people who know them well, such as parents, siblings, teachers, or spouses. Usually they have been convincing enough to gain support and sympathy and sometimes successful at convincing other people that they did nothing wrong. Once they enter the alien territory of the criminal justice system, they have the same objective as always, to convert others to their point of view. Mike was not the least embarrassed or upset when I questioned him about his sexual activities with young boys. In fact, he poured forth more details than I sought. He asserted that what he did benefited the youngsters, and he surmised if I just understood, I would agree. Tad was a young man on the rise, admired by management and, despite his flaws, loved by a loyal and devoted wife. He expected me to conclude that he was not a crook, but a man of good intentions who was just too busy to pay attention to his personal finances.

In psychiatry and psychology, individuals who insist upon being the center of attention are said to have a "narcissistic personality disorder." According to the American Psychiatric Association (APA), among the features of a person with such a "disorder" are the following:[1]

- "A grandiose sense of self-importance"
- "Requires excessive admiration"
- "Has a sense of entitlement"
- "Is interpersonally exploitative"
- "Lacks empathy"
- "Shows arrogant, haughty behaviors or attitudes."

In a discussion of narcissism, the APA manual points out that many extremely successful people appear to have similar features. A "personality disorder" exists only when these traits "are inflexible, maladaptive, and persisting," thereby impairing the person's functioning.

Make no mistake about it! These "narcissists" are victimizers even when their behavior is not illegal. They control people, betray their trust, and use them. As was true with Tad and Mike, they get away with exploitive and often illegal conduct for a long time until they are apprehended.

The loss of control, the fear of what lies ahead, and a threat to the good opinion of the self all may come together so that it begins to dawn on a defendant that the world does not revolve entirely around him. Such a realization may contribute to the defendant at least temporarily abandoning a view that I as his evaluator am just another pawn to be moved about at will. Then he may speak more candidly.

NOTES

1. American Psychiatric Association. *Diagnostic and Statistical Manual of Mental Disorders*. Fourth Edition Text Revision. Arlington, Virginia: American Psychiatric Association, 2000, p. 717.

CHAPTER 16

Six Tactics Used by Defendants to Control Interviews

By now, you know that thinking patterns provide crucial clues to understanding the personalities of people who commit crimes that appear out of character. For most of their lives, these individuals have successfully hidden a great deal of who they are from other people. Their crimes appear out of character in that the behavior is shocking even to those who thought they knew them well. For me to place the crime in a context, to explain the unexplainable, I must come to know intimate aspects of the perpetrator's life in a limited amount of time, an enterprise most defendants do not welcome.

The Larrys, Tads, and Annas do not readily wave a white flag of surrender and tell all. Throughout their lives, they have deployed tactics that have thrown others off track, especially people who have grown perilously close to discovering what they have tried to conceal. Since childhood, they have cased out parents, teachers, neighbors, and anyone else who attempts to hold them accountable. When I come face to face with these defendants in the interview room, I encounter tactics that are so well practiced that they are automatic, just like a sensor that electronically bars entrance to strangers seeking admission to a secure facility.

While trying to figure me out, the defendant is likely to respond warily to questions, volunteering little until he has acquired more information. Initially, a cat and mouse dynamic characterizes our interview.

Two evaluations are in process. I am evaluating the offender, but the offender is evaluating me. Am I a soft touch or a hard liner? Can he sidetrack me by talking about a particular topic in which I might be interested? How concerned does he think I am about whether he likes me? How can he sway me to his point of view? What can he do to convince me of his sincerity? No matter how I approach a defendant, he brings to the evaluation the well practiced and usually successful tactics of a lifetime. I must recognize these tactics and be prepared to deal with them. Otherwise, I risk needlessly antagonizing the defendant, thereby making a difficult job more arduous.

In this chapter, I return to some of the cases which I have already discussed to provide examples of these tactics and how I responded to them. The six tactics are:

- Diversion
- Feeding others what he thinks they want to hear or what they ought to know
- Attempting to confuse others
- Minimization
- Putting others on the defensive
- Building oneself up while putting others down.

As Wally discussed the demise of his marriage and the ensuing custody battle, he sought to convince me that his wife was so malicious, dishonest, and uncaring that she was unfit to raise their son. *Diversion* is a tactic that offenders use in an attempt to shift the focus away from their culpability, usually by focusing on the shortcomings of others. Wally went to extreme lengths to describe Diane's inadequacies and to convince me of her malicious nature. His voice dripping with contempt, Wally said that, as the child custody litigation heated up, Diane "became the best little mommy I ever saw." He maintained that, while he was "bending over backward to tell the truth," Diane was busy at "public relations and building an image." He went on to characterize his ex-wife as "a princess, not a partner," and complained that she would have no part of "being a homemaker." Wally said that if he "had something good going," she would sabotage it, comparing his situation to a pail of crabs, in which one would ruthlessly pull down another that had reached the top of the pile. Wally accused his ex-wife of "digging for dirt" in order to influence a judge. However, during my interviews with him, Wally was doing the same thing, coming up with huge shovels full of dirt in order to bolster his image as the unappreciated father and jilted husband. Wally wanted me to sympathize with his plight so that I could comprehend how he reached the point when he snapped.

I listened patiently to Wally's list of grievances, which constituted a one-sided, extremely self-serving account of his marriage. I inquired as to whether he believed he had contributed to the marital discord. Wally's demeanor changed noticeably, almost as though a dark cloud was passing over the sun, for he hesitated, then commented, "I am pessimistic about your helping me." Translated, this meant that he did not want me to pursue this line of questioning, but instead wanted to continue diverting the discussion to all that was wrong with Diane. By chipping away slowly in a non-confrontational manner, I learned that he picked fights, and that those he didn't start, he fueled by his belligerence and rigidity. Wally acknowledged that he yelled at his wife, threw things, desired to hit her, and "just wanted her out of my life." Having interviewed others who knew Wally and Diane, I asked Wally to respond to what I had learned. For example, I wondered what he thought of observations that he was over-involved with his son Kenny to the point of smothering him. Wally decided not to dispute their opinion. Instead, he used it to point out that the depth of his involvement was necessitated by Diane's negligence and also by an all-consuming fear that she would take Kenny away from him.

A challenge for an interviewer is to give the offender an opportunity to express himself but then to retain a healthy skepticism initially so as not be taken in by explanations that amount to after-the-fact justifications. One listens, then probes in a manner that is not threatening. I wrote earlier about how readily a criminal experiences a sense of being put down. When that occurs, he becomes angry, then wants to assert himself and make his point instead of cooperating. I recognize that when a guy like Wally is set on diverting me from examining him, I do not take him on directly by contesting his assertions that cast blame on other people. Instead, I inquire how he responded to the person or situation that we are discussing. Not just what action did he take, but what does he recall about the thoughts that passed through his mind?

Interviewing Stuart about his rape of a young teenage girl, I wanted to know whether he experienced remorse, an issue I usually explore. The answer is important to understanding the offender's attitude toward what he has done, and it also important to attorneys who hope to present a remorseful client to a judge. Because Stuart had not given any indication that he was remorseful, I commented that I had not heard him speak of the impact of his crime on the girl, her family, friends, or classmates. Stuart took the cue and utilized a tactic that all interviewers of criminal defendants encounter, namely, *feeding others what he thinks they want to hear or what they ought to know.* Without pause, Stuart replied:

I've focused on her and the damage to the house. I wanted to fix the window that was broken. I've thought about her and her parents—about her trust of males, her embarrassment, and her parents' embarrassment in the community.

I asked Stuart if he ever cried, to which he replied that he did. I asked whether he had cried recently, and he responded that he had shed tears at "the idea of my Dad not being able to see me, dying before I get out, losing friends, and my relatives not wanting to accept me as family."

Nothing is unusual about a man in Stuart's situation lamenting his fate even though he was totally responsible for his plight. During a subsequent interview, I asked Stuart what he had been thinking about during the past five days. He replied that his thoughts were of different scenarios in the courtroom, all resulting in a guilty verdict. He commented that he did not like the prospect of "having to look the girl in the face." Stuart made no comment about the girl suffering through the court proceeding, but was very much focused on his own distress.

Sometimes an offender will indicate remorse if he recognizes, then verbalizes his own flaws. Other than the horror of the crime itself and Stuart's years of rape fantasies, the most chilling aspect of the evaluation occurred when I asked if he thought he should change anything about himself. Stuart hesitated as though he had never considered this subject. Knowing that he should come up with something, he replied that he gets impatient, referring to his anxiety about the forthcoming sentencing hearing. He paused again, as though aware he should say more, then commented that he is "too sensitive." Finally, he admitted being at a loss and said, "I don't know if there's something to change."

Throughout many hours of interviewing, Stuart gave little indication that the victim mattered at all. Only when asked specifically about the impact of his crime on the girl did he feed me an answer that he thought would satisfy me and be of value in court.

Perhaps because Larry expressed great remorse over killing his mother, he did not unduly obstruct the flow of information with a barrage of tactics. However, he did present a confusing picture of his relationship with his mother. On the one hand, he emphasized that he was strong-willed and independent. He left his mother and their home to go on numerous dates, to travel to other regions of the country, to shop, and so on. Yet, he also aimed to convince me that his mother was hopelessly dependent and latched onto him so that he lived an abnormally restrictive life.

Attempting to confuse others is a tactic frequently utilized by offenders who want their real motives to remain hidden. Larry commented:

I wanted to be the perfect son. I taught her like I was the father. I know fashion, and I dressed my mother rather well. I couldn't work, take care of her and the household. I couldn't go away. I didn't have time to do homework. I had to do things for her...I'd always do what she said.

As you read these statements, you might think Larry was not attempting to confuse me at all, but was merely giving voice to the pressures he experienced while caring for his mother. When this case went to trial, the defense tried to focus on the terrible predicament Larry was in, how he was psychologically hostage to a needy, clinging, demanding parent from whom he could not extricate himself. The prosecution argued that Larry was trying to confuse the issue by putting the "victim" (i.e., his mother) on trial and blaming her. This was precisely what he and his attorney tried to do—muddy the waters as to who was the victim and who was the victimizer. That approach failed!

Minimization is a tactic that many people, not just criminals, resort to when they want to avoid owning up to what they have done. Offenders do this so frequently that it becomes automatic and often persuasive. While discussing his lifestyle, Fred (the embezzler of a community agency's funds) indicated that he was a big drinker. Because he was vague, I could not determine whether he was an alcoholic. Fred was released on bond during the time I was evaluating him. After "forgetting" one appointment and rescheduling it, he told me that he was not "feeling 100 percent" because, the previous night, he had consumed a half dozen drinks. Explaining that he "got carried away with the group," he used a term that he thought showed psychological insight, for he spoke of capitulating to "peer pressure." Lest I conclude the worst, he assured me, "I don't think I'm an alcoholic." During subsequent appointments, I continued to inquire about his drinking. Two weeks later, he reported downing two mixed drinks at lunch and getting "a real buzz." He also mentioned consuming five beers during a one night drinking bout. During several other interviews, Fred confessed to having had substantial amounts to drink, but he continued to minimize the impact of the alcohol. You might wonder why he admitted to drinking at all when he could have easily lied. From Fred's point of view, he was not in legal hot water for alcohol abuse, so acknowledging alcohol consumption did not seem especially incriminating. To me it was quite relevant! Fred's liberally buying drinks for himself and his dates reflected his extravagance. Alcohol enhanced his "big shot" thinking, fortifying his self-image as the debonair bachelor about town, a gentleman of means, and a magnet to women.

Earlier, I discussed Steven, who, thwarted in his amorous advances to a young woman, abducted her uncle, whom he blamed for the girl's souring attitude toward him. Steven was required by the court to see me for a psychological evaluation. He was not at all pleased at this prospect and seemed determine to fight it. During my first interview, Steven made it clear that he was going to put me through the wringer before I could get anything meaningful out of him. *Putting others on the defensive* is a tactic used by a defendant who decides that, rather than talk about himself, he will put his adversary on the spot and make him the subject of the discussion. Steven focused on my intentions and accused me of being angry, whereas he was the person who was angry even before he walked into my office.

Steven: "I don't know if you're here to help me."

Samenow: "What is your understanding of why you are here?"

Steven: "I don't know why they recommended *you*. I've already opened up to my counselor. I don't open up to somebody unless I trust them. ...I'll be late to work because of this."   [A discussion ensues as to how much time the evaluation will take. Steven says that his supervisor who knows nothing of his legal situation will not permit him to take additional leave. I inform him that I am willing to start at seven in the morning and spread out our sessions so that he will not be late for his job. He ignores the offer and continues to complain.]

Steven: "It's not easy for me to get up. I'm not a morning person." [We have further discussion about the time our meetings will begin, and I offer alternatives. As I try to continue the interview, he shifts the subject to whether I am trustworthy.]

Samenow: "Have you spoken with your girlfriend lately?"

Steven: "I don't want to answer that. I have to trust you first."

Samenow: "What determines whether you trust the person?"

Steven: "How I feel about the person. I look at their personality to see if they want to help me."

Samenow: "What kind of help do you expect from an evaluation such as this one?"

Steven: "To write good things to the court, that I'm not a bad person. You're already upset about my being late....If I refuse, what happens? Do they pick another person?...I don't want to talk about this case over and over."

We reached an impasse as Steven made it clear that he would not answer my questions. I reached for the phone and told him that I would consult his case manager and see what she said. She was emphatic about this evaluation proceeding and asked to speak to Steven. After their conversation, he changed his attitude and said, "I'll tell you the best I can what happened." He cooperated until the beginning of the second meeting when, again, we ground to a standstill as Steven claimed, "I told you everything last time." Again he griped about taking leave but admitted he didn't know how much leave he had. I asked why he did not have that information, to which he retorted irritably, "I don't write it down. I didn't count exactly how much." He said that he could work late, then warned me, "This can happen once or twice, not many times." After this skirmish, Steven finally decided it was best to be done with the whole thing. We spent three hours together, and he was fully cooperative even to the point of scheduling more time without objection.

Like Steven, some defendants think that the best defense is to go on the attack, making me and the process the focus. Because my evaluations are court-ordered or conducted at the request of the defendant's attorney, I encounter this tactic less frequently than the others. Defendants realize that putting the interviewer on the defensive detracts from making a good impression. They don't want to alienate the person who is going to prepare a report and send it to their attorney or to the court.

A more commonly utilized tactic is for the defendant to try to impress the interviewer with his intelligence, talent, sensitivity, and accomplishments. Mary had style and class. Extremely polite and pleasant, she gave every indication that she would fully cooperate. A tactic she used with great skill was to *build herself up while putting others down*. Mary touted her virtues, emphasizing the following:

- She came from a noble southern family lineage that traced itself back to the founding fathers of the United States;
- She was sacrificing a great deal while heroically coping with a husband who was "becoming senile";
- She asserted, "I have spent my life helping people," and provided examples;
- Describing herself as "cultured, poised, elegant, and having a good personality," Mary remarked, "I either inspired jealousy or admiration";
- Mary said that men were constantly falling in love with her: "I had a high IQ, style, I had it all—a fine family background. Men would tell me they were honored to be out with me";
- Although she was charged with drug distribution, Mary proudly declared, "I have never used any illegal drugs, not once."

Mary was so engaging that it was difficult to conceive of this gracious lady as a drug dealer. Her charm was working, or so she thought. It didn't take long before she started to criticize people, making it clear they did not meet her standards. Sometimes she was direct, sometimes subtle. Mary berated her husband and accused him of infidelity and of "treating me like a piece of shit over the years." She expressed contempt for work colleagues and voiced righteous indignation regarding members of the legal system who harassed her and treated her like scum.

Mary's tactic of building herself up had the same purpose as the rest of the tactics that I have described: to remove the focus from her crime. These tactics frequently serve defendants well because they confuse others and throw them off track. A defendant does not have to deliberate about whether to employ these tactics. Because he has utilized them skillfully and frequently, they are like habits that become second nature

CHAPTER 17

Secret Controllers: Several Cases

*A*ll of the defendants described above were intelligent, accomplished, articulate, and talented. They were so adept at controlling others that their tremendous need to be in control usually went unnoticed. The people who knew them were so smitten with the positive aspects of their personalities and their achievements that any minuses were considered to be idiosyncrasies or rough edges. It is not unusual for people to make allowances for the egotism of bright, high achievers. Larry, Wally, Mary, Fred, and the others whom I have discussed were uncompromising in pursuing their objectives. They successfully hid the dark aspects of their personalities. Let me now give you thumbnail sketches of two other secret controllers whose crimes seemed out of character but were anything but.

Thomas inspired others by overcoming obstacles as he rose from poverty, earned a doctoral degree from a top university, and became a professional educator. When I first met him, he was escorted into my office in handcuffs and leg irons by sheriff's deputies who transported him from jail. Thomas had been charged with homicide, having shot to death a man who had been his wife's lover. The judge who presided at the hearing where a jury found him guilty stated that letters received from his colleagues and friends described him as "an exemplary citizen" without so much as a parking ticket. I was to evaluate him prior to sentencing.

By no means unwilling to toot his own horn, Thomas told me that he personified the American dream, rising from an impoverished childhood similar to that of Elvis Presley. He worked indefatigably until he reached a position of power and influence. Not only did others affirm that Thomas had acted out of character in shooting his wife's paramour, but Thomas himself asserted that what he had done "is totally antithetical to my behavior." He claimed, "I don't belong in jail. There were two victims—[the man he shot] and my career. You've read my vita. Why did this happen to me? I'm still in shock."

From what Thomas related and by reading the testimonial letters written on his behalf to the judge, I learned that he was widely respected and admired. After boasting about his accomplishments, Thomas told me, "I'm a humble person, a modest person." He was outraged that any judge would even consider incarcerating him.

To be locked up with people who are unable to reason as well as I can.... You have very few highly intelligent people, people I'm comfortable relating to. There's a bell-shaped curve. People who are mediocre and degenerates, they have to derive their sense of being by persecuting others.

In one area of life, the usually confident Thomas had lost control and felt extremely vulnerable. His marriage, which had been deteriorating, reached a critical point. His wife repeatedly said that she would leave and return to her hometown. It seemed to Thomas that she might actually make good on this threat. Asked why the marital relationship had gone down hill, Thomas first was vague.

There was a change in the authority in the family. I sensed an independence on my wife's part. She wanted to be more than my wife....I wanted to restore the marriage to what I thought I had. I developed problems of intense jealousy and anger....It became clear that I wasn't wanted, but I held on hoping things would be better.

The key phrase to me was "a change in authority." When I asked what that meant, Thomas indicated that he was no longer in charge. His wife, long subservient, had become fed up with his domination of their relationship and wanted to be treated as a partner. This was more than Thomas could endure.

She felt she couldn't actualize her potential in our marriage. She felt I was overprotective...She'd use terms like "imprisoned." In her view, I disallowed her freedom. The more frustrated I became, the more questions

I asked. The relationship started off with my being domineering. I controlled the money. I wouldn't allow her a checking or savings account. In the last few years, it seemed as though our joint decision making wasn't working. She was making the decisions....She made personal decisions about where and when she wanted to go. It was the opposite of what we had done. There were new rules.

Thomas said that their love life had gone downhill because, as with other aspects of their relationship, she was not satisfying him. In a revealing statement, Thomas commented, "Either you satisfy my needs, or I cannot be affectionate to you."

It was clear that Thomas, who described himself as a mover and shaker in his professional life, was anything but that at home. His wife's increasing assertiveness left him "emotionally strained beyond my limit." He expained, "I love myself. I have a high self-concept. I'm self-actualized. I don't need problems like I've had. I'm a proud person. I could do just about anything I want to."

Thomas said that he could not get his wife to change her behavior. The greatest threat to his ego was his wife showing interest in other men, especially the person with whom he believed she was having an affair. This is the man whom he gunned down.

During my career as a forensic psychologist, I have had a number of cases in which a person who was successful in his career became accustomed to having subordinates do his bidding. However, in an intimate relationship, he lacked the power and constant acclaim that nourished his self-image. When his partner eluded his control, she or someone she was involved with paid with their life.

· · · · ·

Barbara was a senior sales executive for a large high-tech corporation. She also was a wife and mother of two children. She was arrested in the parking lot of a department store for possessing clothing that she shoplifted. Charged with grand larceny, she spent most of the day in jail and, at first, was too embarrassed even to call her husband. Once she was released on bond, Barbara came to see me at the request of her attorney. Although she had no criminal record, she confessed immediately that her shoplifting, which seemed so totally out of character, had been a part of her life for "as far back as I can remember." Her first memory of stealing was pilfering candy from a store at age four.

As busy as Barbara was with her career and family, she would plan each day around going to the store. She estimated that she had shoplifted nearly $10,000 worth of merchandise during the past year, yet was apprehended only this one time for taking a few expensive items. Barbara observed that it became "so habitual to steal" that it was a "no brainer" to do it. She became a pro! Because at work she was a supervisor with a lot of authority, no one questioned her comings and goings. "I had a lot of freedom," she observed. Once in a while, Barbara had considered getting help but didn't because she believed therapy was "mumbo jumbo." Her husband Drew knew nothing of her shoplifting. She told me that he trusted her because she had been faithful and done "all the wifey things." Because she earned a lot of money, Drew didn't question how she acquired any specific item. He knew better than to question his wife about anything she did. In the marital relationship, Barbara was in control. She expected Drew to take on faith whatever she said. Barbara had her way, or Drew paid a price of enduring her searing anger or cold silence.

Before meeting Drew, Barbara's conduct had not been so stellar. She said that she "bounced checks right and left," ran up debt, and had her car repossessed. As a teenager, she had used illegal drugs and had been sexually promiscuous. Drew knew nothing about any of this. Barbara commented that, because of her arrest, "My husband must wonder 'what do I have here?'"

Barbara marveled that she had been so slick that neither Drew nor her work colleagues had caught on to her. At work she had a reputation as an extremely competent, "take charge" person. She had "received so many accolades" that others thought she could do no wrong. Barbara figured that no one would really care, much less question her, if she failed to show up at all on any given day. "I was perfect; everyone thought I was perfect," she observed. Although this might reflect a strikingly conceited view of herself, Barbara had the situation sized up quite well. No one questioned what she did.

At home, Barbara did what she had to, although she seethed with discontent and frustration. She resented all the responsibility and left the bulk of the daily chores to Drew. She complained to me that marriage was "boring." But with Drew as her virtual slave, she had resolved to stick with him. Barbara wanted to enjoy her children but leave the details of their care to Drew. She acknowledged that her children paid a price having a mother who didn't like being a mother. The girls didn't conform to her expectations and needed more attention than she wanted to provide. Consequently, she was a yeller and a spanker because, as Barbara put it, she didn't like being "inconvenienced" by her children.

When I interviewed Drew, he had been concerned for a long time about his wife's increasing irritability and lashing out at the children. He said, "They badger her for something. She erupts, yells at them or me too and says she's had enough. Her reaction is out of proportion."

Drew was shocked when Barbara told him that she had been stealing most of her life. When he asked why, Barbara replied that it "gave her some feeling of power." I asked if he had come to have a different view of his wife. Drew replied that she still was the faithful and basically truthful person he had married. He said, "I have 99 percent the same trust and confidence I had before this. I don't trust her any less." Drew commented, "People are so impressed with Barbara. She is an amazing person." Apparently, Barbara counted on her husband being supportive. This was how it had always been. Whatever indiscretion she might commit, people overlooked it and forgave her. She said of Drew, "He doesn't dwell on things. He treats me as if nothing happened. He accepted me again for me." Nothing much changed. Barbara remained in control of her husband, her children, and her work situation. Her authority remained unchallenged!

· · · · ·

A NOTORIOUS SECRET CONTROLLER: WASHINGTON, D.C. SNIPER LEE BOYD MALVO

During September and October of 2002, two men terrorized a heavily populated region extending from Baltimore, Maryland, to Richmond, Virginia. John Allen Muhammad and Lee Boyd Malvo shot 13 people, including a 13-year-old boy. Ten victims died. Complete strangers to Muhammad and Malvo, these individuals were just going about their daily lives. As the homicides shattered the security of millions, people worried that they, their families, friends, or neighbors might be next to die at the hands of the anonymous killer or killers. Schools were on lockdown as outdoor recreation, athletic, and other events were held indoors or cancelled. People hurried to complete routine daily tasks lest they find themselves in the line of fire. They nervously looked around when they got out of their cars or walked from one place to another. With Halloween approaching, there was talk of canceling festivities, including banning trick-or-treating. Such precautions became unnecessary as the two men were finally arrested on October 24, 2005, asleep in their parked car. The state of Virginia was the first to try Muhammad and Malvo, even though they also had committed homicides in other locations, including Maryland and the District of Columbia. The trials of both men were moved from the Washington, D.C., area to Virginia Beach for Mr. Muhammad and to Chesapeake for Mr. Malvo. Before Malvo went on trial, a jury found Muhammad guilty of capital murder and sentenced him to death.

I was appointed by Robert Horan, the Fairfax County Commonwealth's Attorney, to evaluate Mr. Malvo's mental condition on October 14, 2002, when he shot Linda Franklin to death while she was in a parking lot outside a Home Depot in the Seven Corners (Virginia) Shopping Center. Lee Malvo's legal defense team asserted that he was insane at the time he committed the crime. Like Anna in chapter 7, Lee Malvo was said to have suffered from a "Dissociative Disorder." The defense asserted that, having suffered deprivation and abuse as a child, Mr. Malvo was needy and vulnerable to outside influence. The attorneys argued that Lee Malvo was dominated by John Muhammad and indoctrinated so that he was not himself when he participated in the shootings. In effect, the attorneys were arguing that Mr. Malvo's murderous conduct was completely out of character for a person with no criminal record and whose primary trait had been obedience.

I spent approximately 34 hours interviewing Lee Malvo while he was incarcerated at two detention centers. The information about Mr. Malvo that I am citing here is a matter of public record either in court transcripts from testimony that I and others provided at his capital murder trial or in media coverage.

Mr. Malvo was polite and cooperative. In fact, he was one of the easiest defendants to talk to that I had ever encountered. The evaluation assumed more of a conversational style than a question and answer format. Just 17 years old, Mr. Malvo indicated that he was well-read as he alluded to writings of Spinoza and other philosophers. He said that if he could have access to more books in jail, he would immerse himself in philosophy all day. Deploring a lack of worthwhile reading matter,

Mr. Malvo stated that he had taken to reading the dictionary. Lee Malvo expressed pride in being self-disciplined with respect to diet and exercise even while incarcerated.

Despite the ease I experienced in speaking with Mr. Malvo, the defendant made it clear that he was on guard and extremely well-versed as to the nature of the legal proceedings. When I inquired as to whether my being appointed by the prosecution affected his responses, Mr. Malvo indicated that nothing intimidates him, including the possibility that he might be put to death. He warned me that some personal matters he shares with nobody. He would determine what was appropriate for discussion and asserted that he did not have to explain himself to anybody. When we approached a topic he wanted to declare off limits, Mr. Malvo would chide me for asking, indicating we should move on to another topic. Despite his personal charm and responsiveness, Lee Malvo intended to remain in control.

Mr. Malvo adhered to the theme that formed the nucleus of his defense, namely that he participated in the shootings owing to circumstances not within his control. Calculatingly, he made statements to bolster his legal defense that he was shaped by a horrendous childhood and later by John Muhammad. However, in response to my questioning, he directly contradicted these assertions by providing evidence that he affected others perhaps even more than they affected him. Lee Malvo proclaimed that he was a unique and fearless individual: "There's not much I fear...I wouldn't want to be like anyone else. I like me. There's nobody like me. I like uniqueness."

Born in Kingston, Jamaica, Lee Boyd Malvo lived with his biological parents until he was five years old, at which time his mother and father separated. Two years later, his mother, Una James, no longer allowed him to have any relationship with his father, Leslie Malvo. At the age of 10, Mr. Malvo encountered his father by chance and asked if he could live with him. He recalled being devastated when his dad turned him down ostensibly because he lived on another island six months a year working as a contractor. Mr. Malvo's lawyers emphasized the impact on Lee Malvo of losing his father, then searching for a father figure, which he found in Mr. Muhammad. In contrast, Mr. Malvo told me that not having a father involved in a youngster's daily life was commonplace in the country and culture in which he lived. Asked whether he had friends who also had no relationship with their father, Mr. Malvo replied, speaking in general terms about Jamaican blacks, "More than 90 percent of us don't have a father." He pointed out that it is exceptional for black family units to remain intact in Jamaica. Mr. Malvo said that, despite lacking a father, several close friends had turned out well and were attending college.

Mental health professionals for the defense cited the adverse impact on Lee Malvo of being raised by an erratic, unstable, and sometimes harsh mother who frequently deserted him and farmed him out to live with others. Mr. Malvo said that his mother was constantly lecturing him about his misbehavior and administering extreme punishments, including beatings, for minor infractions. When I asked about the use of corporal punishment in Jamaica, Mr. Malvo told me that it is very common, not just at home but also in school. He referred to the school principal's office as "a slaughterhouse." He observed that a child might get whipped twice for the same infraction, once when it happened (by a teacher or another adult) and then again at home.

Despite his mother's strictness and unpredictability, Lee Malvo recalled wanting her to stay with him. Una James maintained she could not afford to remain, that she had to leave Jamaica so she could work and earn more to support her son. Mr. Malvo said that many of his friends had mothers who did exactly the same thing because jobs were hard to find in Jamaica, and high inflation eroded the value of earnings. Lee Malvo went to an extreme to convince his mother to stay when he stood on a stool, wrapped a sheet around a mango tree, then slipped a noose around his neck. For two hours, Ms. James talked to her son, promising to see if she could remain at home with him, all the while warning that a person who commits suicide goes to hell. Lee backed down; he thought he had achieved what he wanted!

Mr. Malvo resented any attempt to portray his mother as a villain. Despite all the difficulties he had with her, Lee Malvo said that she "did a darn good job" and "did the best with what she had." He was aware that she believed in his potential, and all her dreams rested on him. Una James never wavered from her insistence on her son becoming well-educated in order to have a better life than she did. So concerned was Ms. James about her son's education that she'd frequently call whatever school he was attending to check on his attendance and academic progress. She worked hard to earn the funds to place Lee in good schools, including a facility that required him to reside in a boarding home. In a newspaper interview, Ms. James remarked, "If I were a wicked mother, would I earn my living and spend it on him?"[1] Mr. Malvo told me that during some summers, when everyone else was having fun, his mother had him toiling at academics. Although she bought video games for her son, Una James insisted on being physically present to supervise his playing them. When Lee lived at the boarding home, he would sneak out to an arcade where he would spend hours playing videogames. Growing bored with adventure games, he turned to games that involved violence and killing.

At one point, Una James left her son in the care of a widower, Theodore Williams. Despite having a good relationship with this man, Mr. Malvo left Mr. Williams' home and lived on his own. His mother's influence remained strong even in her absence. Lee never missed school, because he knew she would call to check on him. He continued to perform well enough academically so that school authorities never suspected he was without adult supervision.

Because of his difficult childhood, Lee Malvo was seen as vulnerable to adverse influences. In newspaper accounts and in court testimony, he was described as so "needy" and "malleable" that he could be easily "brainwashed," "dominated," "indoctrinated," "programmed," turned into "a puppet," and turned into "a child soldier" as he came "under the spell of" John Allen Muhammad. The defense asserted that Malvo turned into a different person: "Lee Malvo was gone."[2] Throughout my interviews, Lee Malvo did not corroborate that portrayal. Mr. Malvo made it clear that, even as a young boy, he had an extremely willful personality. Headstrong and defiant even in small ways, he risked receiving severe punishment by his mother and other caretakers, punishment at school, and engendering hostility from his peers.

Lee Malvo volunteered that he was also "a control freak." Being in control at all times, no matter what the situation, was so important that Mr. Malvo did not even want to be under the influence of any sort of medication and refused to take any, even if prescribed for an illness. He knew that good health was a prerequisite to almost anything else. His emphasis on vitamins, minerals, and physical fitness preceded meeting Mr. Muhammad.

As a young child, Lee would stand up to anyone! He recalled rebelling against doing chores while living with a friend of his mother's and her husband:

I'd come home and have to wash dishes and do chores. I said, "I ain't doing this. I've been at school all day. That's my job..." A lot of times I didn't wash them. He could beat me until God came home, and he did...Either I wouldn't do them properly or I'd take so long. Then I'd say "no."

Although many youngsters might balk when asked to do chores, Lee Malvo would dig in his heels and refuse to capitulate, no matter what the consequence. He recalled that if he didn't see a sound reason for being told to do something, he refused to cooperate. He was his own authority. About boarding home rules, he said, "They made a rule; I broke it."

Mr. Malvo attempted to dominate peers. When he hung out at the community center, no matter what subject was being discussed, Lee knew more than anyone. He would openly express contempt for others' opinions and wasn't bashful about telling them blatantly that they had no idea what they were talking about. During classroom discussions, he belittled contemporaries, especially if the subjects concerned current events or religion. He boasted that between the ages of 10 and 14, he and several friends "ruled the class." School records are replete with notations that Lee did not work up to potential. He had both stellar grades and failing grades. If he found a subject of interest, he gave it his all. Otherwise, he considered school boring, didn't do the work, and was seen as having a "lackadaisical attitude." Mr. Malvo challenged teachers, insisting that his point of view or interpretation of subject matter was the only accurate one. He'd flout authority, get admonished, then play the innocent victim. Mr. Malvo claimed that he and several classmates drove off more than a dozen teachers in a single term, then intimidated the Prefect so he did not report their misconduct.

At Mr. Malvo's trial, teachers testified as to what a good student he was and praised him for obedience. Unquestionably, in classes numbering as many as 55 students, Lee stood out for his intellectual promise and accomplishment. Mr. Malvo counted on impressing teachers so that he could get away with misconduct that would not have been tolerated if engaged in by fellow students.

Lee Malvo stated that once his mind locks onto any objective, he "zones out" so that nothing else matters. He is then absolutely certain that he will succeed at whatever he undertakes. Mr. Malvo recalled going all out whenever he played a competitive sport: "losing wasn't an option." Lee referred to himself as "stubborn," a reference to the pride he took in having a will of iron. He rejected pleas by his mother to stay with her once she had a more stable situation. Her warning about John Muhammad, "He'll take you to your death. He's no good," fell on deaf ears.

Lee Malvo's mother and teachers instilled in him a concept of right and wrong. When it came to pursuing what he wanted, Lee cast this teaching aside. Before becoming involved with Mr. Muhammad in the sniper shootings, Lee Malvo had committed numerous crimes and shown a penchant for violence. At five, he convinced his mother to get him a cat. They discovered that, contrary to what they had been told, the animal had never been trained. When the cat defecated all over the house, including on Lee's bed, Una James took her anger out on Lee and whipped him. From then on, Lee chased the cat out of the house with a broom every time it showed up. Then he shot marbles at feral cats, using a metal catapult to kill the animals. Mr. Malvo estimated that he had stunned nearly 30 and killed a dozen. At age seven, he repeatedly stole money from his mother. As a young boy, Mr. Malvo amassed a collection of hundreds of comic books. He and two friends frequently purchased comics at a store. Taking advantage of being trusted as regular customers, they pilfered dozens of comic books during a two-year period. He and some buddies also stole compact disc recordings, which they resold for a third less than retail price. Mr. Malvo calculatingly limited the amount he deposited in his bank account, because his mother kept careful track of how much should be in it. "Opportunity showed itself," Mr. Malvo recalled, citing an occasion when a friend stole an unattended bag of cash lying on a cash register, and the two split the proceeds consisting of 7,000 Jamaican dollars.

Lee Malvo was no stranger to violence. For two years, he waited for an opportunity to strike back at a boy who had bullied him. He had his chance to retaliate when he spotted his adversary walking alone to school. When the youngster called him a name, Lee attacked: "I sucker punched him. I had a good start. I kept pounding his fuckin' ass....He didn't know I'd actually stand up to him to fight." Mr. Malvo said that, although he usually remains calm, he will take "drastic steps" when he gets angry. He knew that someone had been swiping food out of his lunch bag for almost a month. Lee warned his classmates that if he discovered the identity of the thief, that person would pay dearly. When he finally spotted the culprit, he waited for the bell to ring, then took his revenge: "I picked up a drum, a garbage can and beat him with it. . . . When I snap, I snap. . . . You wouldn't want to be the person I snapped on." Mr. Malvo took pride in the fact that even close friends feared his temper.

Spending his early years in Kingston, Mr. Malvo said he constantly heard gun fire and often saw dead bodies on the street. Frightened and perplexed by the violence around him, he developed a keen interest in firearms and, by age seven, could distinguish one weapon from another. Mr. Malvo's longstanding fascination with guns was reflected in a drawing made in jail of 11 different firearms which he labeled by type. During an interview by Detective Boyle of the Fairfax County Police Department, Lee Malvo remarked, "Snipers adore their weapons."[3]

The defense contended that Mr. Malvo met John Muhammad when he was a vulnerable adolescent. One newspaper account characterized Lee Malvo's transformation under Mr. Muhammad's influence as being comparable to "a polluted river overwhelming a pristine stream."[4] In a nutshell, their case was that Lee Boyd Malvo was so dominated and "brainwashed" that he became unable to differentiate right from wrong. The prosecution vehemently disagreed, argued that Malvo and Muhammad were like "peas in a pod," and dismissed the insanity defense as a "smokescreen."

Lee's intellectual interests and life experiences prepared him to embrace what John Muhammad had to offer. Well before he met Mr. Muhammad, Lee had grown impassioned over social injustice, especially mistreatment of blacks, and had read extensively on this subject.

Lee Malvo met John Muhammad at an electronics shop in Antigua where Mr. Muhammad was playing video games with his son. (Lee's mother already knew Mr. Mohammad as a person who might help her obtain false documents so that she could travel to the United States.) The teenager and the man began conversing, and Mr. Muhammad bought Lee ice cream. Thereafter, Mr. Malvo began hanging around him during free time, often visiting his home after school. Once Lee began living on his own, he asked Mr. Muhammad if he could move in with him and, in

January 2001 did just that. He was gratified that Mr. Muhammad seemed to support his desire to attend college and took seriously his ambition to become a pilot.

Lee Malvo portrayed himself to me as a person who had his own ideas and who could not be pushed around by anyone. Believing that his peers were ill-informed, he was not inclined to be led by them. Mr. Malvo claimed to be a skeptic, an individual who did his own fact finding. Occasionally during the evaluation, Mr. Malvo fortified the central theme of his legal defense by claiming that he became subservient to John Muhammad. However, the main thrust of his statements indicated that his mind was not a blank slate for Mr. Muhammad's indoctrination. Rather, Mr. Muhammad's teachings fell on already fertile soil. Mr. Malvo declared to me, "I'm not impressionable. I'm not weak-minded."

When John Muhammad was arrested during March 2001 for fraudulent activities, Lee was ready to fill his shoes. He moved Muhammad's three children to a safe location that had been selected in advance in case the police showed up. No longer attending school, Lee became the instructor for Mr. Muhammad's offspring. Mr. Malvo had been keenly observant of Mr. Muhammad's enterprises and was able to quickly take over forging American birth certificates and obtaining passports. For delivering these documents, Mr. Malvo earned $14,000 in two months. When Mr. Muhammad was released, he took Lee with him to the United States, and the pair stayed with Mr. Muhammad's friends in Ft. Lauderdale, Florida.

Upon learning that her son was living with John Muhammad, Una James, then residing in Florida, became extremely concerned. Lee went to live with his mother in Ft. Myers, Florida, where he spent the summer and enrolled in school, all the while clandestinely maintaining frequent phone contact with Mr. Muhammad. In October, Mr. Malvo ran off to join Mr. Muhammad, navigating his way across the United States to Bellingham, Washington. Lee continued to stay in touch with his mother by phoning her regularly. As stubborn and determined as her son was, Una James was equally determined. She traveled to Washington, determined Lee's whereabouts, contacted the police, and sought their assistance, telling them that her son was in danger. The police detained both mother and son, Lee in a juvenile detention center in Spokane, his mother in a jail in Seattle. Upon release, Lee was placed in his mother's custody. Una James appealed to Lee to live with her, indicating that she could acquire legal status for both of them in the United States and that she would send him to school. Lee wasn't persuaded and again ran away to join Mr. Muhammad. When I asked why he left, Mr. Malvo was at a loss for an explanation, stating, "I wish I could explain it." He then said that he feared his mother might get deported. He also believed that, because she worried so about his safety, she would not help him become a pilot.

Whereas most people, upon discovering what John Muhammad was really like, would have fled, Lee Malvo found more and more to admire. Mr. Malvo knew that Mr. Muhammad's immediate objective was to locate his children, then living in the custody of their mother, and remove them from the United States. The larger cause, or "the mission," as Mr. Malvo called it, was to create a utopian society for black children in Canada. Lee Malvo fully supported this objective as it appeared to be a step toward improving the plight of blacks.

As the two began the mission, traveling across the United States, Mr. Malvo occasionally grew apprehensive. He managed his anxiety by doing what he always had done—consciously making an effort to eliminate emotion and focus exclusively on what must be accomplished. The first time Lee Malvo saw Mr. Muhammad kill a person, he realized that he had a lot "more work to do" on himself before he could do the same thing. Asked if he had shot people as Mr. Muhammad had before the Washington, D.C., shootings, Mr. Malvo laughed and admonished me about even thinking he would answer such a question. Once Lee shot someone, he found that he developed much better control of his emotions and could talk himself out of being afraid. Occasionally, Mr. Muhammad left Lee by himself. At such times, he could have gone off on his own. Instead, Mr. Malvo became increasingly committed to their joint enterprise.

To obtain funds for the mission, Malvo and Muhammad engaged in scams and robberies, some at gunpoint. The Washington, D.C., metropolitan area was selected as the focus because, according to Mr. Malvo, it was "the capital of the world," and people everywhere would sit up and take notice. It was also the area in which Mr. Muhammad's children lived with their mother.

Mr. Malvo described the meticulous manner in which he and John Muhammad operated. Lee was explicit about his method of conducting reconnaissance for each of the shootings. According to a news report, Mr. Malvo told a correctional officer at a Maryland jail, "Before I went out killing people, I didn't eat. You get more oxygen to the brain and stay more alert."[5] As a "spotter," it was his job to calculate the wind speed as well as the distance between himself and the targeted person. Having the police in the vicinity was no deterrent. In fact, it added to the challenge. After his arrest, Lee Malvo told a detective, "I make you move and then I see what you do and then I strategize and beat you."[6] Mr. Malvo acknowledged being the trigger man in all of the shootings. One might wonder about why Lee Malvo would kill a black man while deploring mistreatment of blacks. Mr. Malvo explained it did not matter who was killed, whether the person was black or white, young or old. While shooting, he placed himself psychologically in the "zone," referring to his ability to single-mindedly carry out the "mission" and shut off undesirable emotions and thoughts.

Malvo and Muhammad not only played cat and mouse with the police as they maneuvered and carried out the shootings, but they also verbally taunted law enforcement officials throughout their spree. One newspaper reported, "The snipers tried to tease the police with clumsy clues."[7] On the evening of October 18, 2002, a Catholic priest said he received a phone call from two people "claiming to have knowledge of the shootings and who provided details thereof which, until that time, were known only to law enforcement."[8] At the site of the October 19 shooting in Ashland, Virginia, Malvo left a note demanding $10 million from the government in exchange for which the killings would cease. In a postscript, he warned, "Your children are not safe anywhere anytime." On an illustration drawn for police, Mr. Malvo wrote, "September 11 we will ensure will look like a picnic to you."[9] A defense psychiatrist noted that Muhammad had selected more than 100 possible shooting sites in the Washington area "to keep the authorities not knowing where the next shooting was going to occur."[10]

Mr. Malvo said that he and Muhammad were caught because they grew "lazy," a reference to letting down their guard and falling asleep in their vehicle at a parking area. When he was initially jailed in Maryland, Lee Malvo was not in the least subdued. Breaking a table leg that he was handcuffed to, he unsuccessfully tried to escape through a ceiling tile. Mr. Malvo commented, "As long as I'm alive, I'm going home or die trying."

Lee Boyd Malvo was diagnosed by defense mental health professionals as suffering from a "dissociative disorder, not otherwise specified." According to the Diagnostic and Statistical Manual of the American Psychiatric Association, the "not otherwise specified" phrase means that there is "a dissociative symptom that does not meet the criteria for any specific Dissociative Disorder."[11] One example provided is "states of dissociation that occur in individuals who have been subjected to periods of prolonged and intense coercive persuasion" with "brainwashing" specifically mentioned. In his book on dissociative identify disorder, Dr. Colin Ross noted that the entire concept of dissociation "fell into disrepute" during the late nineteenth century but, since 1980, has made a comeback.[12] He speculated that the concept might again fall into disrepute. Dr. Ross pointed out, "It makes sense to fake dissociative disorder when charged with crimes, only if that is a good legal strategy."

Throughout my evaluation, Lee Malvo emphasized that he not only controlled other people from the time he was very young, but that he also had an enormous sense of control and power while slaughtering innocent individuals who were doing nothing other than living their day-to-day lives. Deliberately and habitually, Lee Malvo was able to shut off from awareness any thought or emotion that might interfere with achieving an objective. Through his relationship with John Muhammad, Mr. Malvo sharpened this mental process. John Muhammad was a mentor to a very willing student.

Concluding their deliberations shortly before Christmas, the jury in Chesapeake, Virginia, found Lee Malvo guilty of capital murder. The insanity defense failed. After deliberating nearly 14 hours, the jury sentenced him to life in prison without parole. His youthfulness at the time of the shooting figured in sparing him a death sentence. (On March 1, 2005, the U.S. Supreme Court ruled that a juvenile cannot be sentenced to death.)

John Muhammad was convicted of first degree murder during a 2006 trial in Montgomery County, Maryland. Mr. Malvo was a witness at that proceeding. Before the trial commenced, he told law enforcement officials that, before the Washington, D.C., slayings, he and Mr. Muhammad had participated in four additional shootings in which two victims died.[13]

(These were in addition to homicides the pair were known to have committed in Washington, Alabama, and Louisiana.) In all, Lee Malvo and John Muhammad shot 27 people, 17 of whom died.

Two diametrically opposite views were presented of this young man at his trial. One was of a weak, needy person who became psychologically enslaved by an older and very powerful (to some people, evil) man. The other was of a smart and wily youth who found in John Muhammad not a father but a co-conspirator. One could speculate that if Lee Malvo had never met John Muhammad, perhaps he would not have been involved in sniper attacks directed toward total strangers. But Mr. Malvo still had the personality and thinking errors of a secret controller. Those characteristics were being expressed increasingly in antisocial conduct well before he met Mr. Muhammad.

NOTES

1. "Malvo's Mother Defends Strict Parenting, Beatings,"*The Washington Post*, December 14, 2003, p. C6.

2. "Malvo's Case in Hands of Jury," *The Washington Post*, December 17, 2003, p. A30

3. Transcript of interview of Lee Malvo by Detective June Boyle, Fairfax County (Va.) Police Department.

4. "Malvo Guilty of Capital Murder," *The Washington Post*, December 19, 2003, p. A 30.

5. "Malvo's Restless Journey For Belonging and Direction," *The Washington Post*, November 9, 2003, p. A12.

6. Transcript of Interview of Lee Malvo by Detective Sam Walker of the Prince William County (Va.) Police Department, November 8, 2002, p. 25.

7. "Cat and Mouse," *Newsweek*, November 4, 2002, p. 36.

8. Affidavit in Support of Application for Search Warrant, October 25, 2003.

9. "Malvo Jury Hears Pleas For Justice, Compassion," *The Washington Post*, December 23, 2003, p. B4.

10. "Disparities in Malvo's Interviews Questioned," *The Washington Post*, December 12, 2003, p. B. 5.

11. American Psychiatric Association. *Diagnostic and Statistical Manual of Mental Disorder,* Fourth Edition Text Revision, Arlington, Va.: American Psychiatric Association, 2000, p. 532.

12. Ross, Colin. *Dissociative Identity Disorder,* NY: Wiley, 1997.

13. "Malvo Claims 4 Other Shootings, Source Says," *The Washington Post,* June 16, 2006, p. A1.

CHAPTER 18

Can a Person Correct Thinking Errors?

*T*he older we are, the more ingrained habits become. This is certainly the case with errors in thinking. Even if a person is determined to eliminate old patterns, no matter what they are, change seldom happens quickly. If an individual is sufficiently motivated, change is possible. To change any longstanding habit, a person must become convinced that it has been self-destructive and harmful to people whom he cares about. Sometimes people make changes just to get others to stop pressuring them. Such compliance is a token measure and not the same as basic and enduring change.

I meet with offenders when they are no longer in control. They have been stopped in their tracks and are facing the prospect of severe limitations on their freedom. Some have alienated their most ardent supporters and admirers. When I evaluate them, they are dissatisfied more with their situations than they are with themselves. From time to time, I function not as an evaluator but as a counselor. I meet with offenders, adults and juveniles, who are referred to me by courts, schools, and social service agencies, or are dragged to me by parents, spouses, or other family members. The hope is that I can help the offender become a responsible human being.

There are two sources for motivation: external circumstances and internal factors. The first is critical. An extremely negative event, such as an arrest or incarceration, must get the offender's attention so that he understands that, if he continues on the same path, worse consequences eventually will follow. No matter how grim the situation, no threat by an authority or anyone else can compel someone to change against his will. For meaningful and lasting change to occur, the offender eventually must develop motivation within himself to look in the mirror and dislike what he sees. External leverage can assist in bringing him to this point, especially if he knows that he could have probation revoked, be subject to relocation to a different and perhaps worse facility, or experience the withdrawal of support by those who have stood by him. As I meet with an offender, I am asking that he do what no one likes to do—come face to face with his shortcomings. Part of my task is to help generate internal motivation, to help the offender become fed up with himself.

This process usually begins after the offender has been arrested, while he copes with the uncertainty as to what the outcome in court will be. Understandably, his primary motivation is to get out of the jam he has created for himself. Some offenders, however, begin thinking about what brought them to this predicament and contemplate what may be a dismal future. The early meetings may begin while the offender is in the local jail surrounded by the consequences of his crime. In other instances, I may begin work with the individual in the community while he is awaiting trial or after he is on probation. During the early meetings, I discuss what a videotape of his daily life would reveal. His arrest may appear to have resulted from an "out of character" crime. I know that it represents the tip of an iceberg. Without going into the details of past offenses, I discuss patterns of irresponsibility and illegal activity that we would see on the hypothetical videotape. Two profound questions provide the underpinning to our conversations: "What kind of person are you? What kind of person do you want to be?"

I began work with Phillip just after he was released from jail and placed on probation. (His ever-hopeful family learned about me from Phillip's probation officer and was willing to pay for my services.) Now in his thirties, Phillip had thrown away more opportunities than some people ever have. The crimes for which he was originally sentenced were setting small fires in which, fortunately, no one was hurt. These were seen by his family as completely out of character. Phillip had no history even as a child of playing with matches.

I quickly found that counseling Phillip on an outpatient basis was like trying to catch a tidal wave with a bucket. Within two months, his probation was revoked when he was apprehended for stealing. Refusing to give up on their son, his parents asked me to continue working with him in jail. What followed was nearly two years of meetings with Phillip while he was incarcerated. I had his attention! In a more restrictive environment, he was far more cooperative and truthful than he had been. I asked him to write notes about incidents that occurred and to try to remember and write down thoughts that he had at the time. It took a while for him to understand what this meant. Phillip was accustomed to doing whatever he wanted without questioning himself. Scrutinizing his own thinking was not natural.

Jail was to serve as his arena for change. Anything could be a topic for discussion: interactions with other inmates, contacts with correctional officers, a visit from his mother, a letter from a girlfriend. Far more happened than we had time to discuss. But Phillip did his homework, jotting down events that had occurred and recording not only what he said and did, but what he thought about saying and doing. We would focus on an event or a thought, then discuss what it revealed about him. The objective was to increase his awareness of the destruction he had left in his wake and how it affected even people whom he professed to care about, especially his family. Among topics arising with considerable frequency were anger at other inmates, frustration with corrections staff, anger at a girlfriend who ceased writing, resentment of a sister who refused to visit or write, and fantasies about female inmates whom he tried to befriend at Bible classes.

Phillip seemed to take to this process much better than he did when he was on probation. Skeptics, including his own attorney, wondered if he was just playing along, feeding me what he thought I wanted to hear, something that this smooth talking young man was quite good at. His exhausted family continued to hope for the best, but also feared that perhaps he was not sincere. Indicators that Phillip was making an effort included his volunteering an increasing number of incidents and thoughts. If the gap between sessions lasted more than a week, he began mailing to me the notes he made about his thoughts. Becoming more realistic in his expectations of others in his environment, he complained less and was not so angry. He read *Inside the Criminal Mind* and *Before It's Too*

Late, two books that I had written, making notes as to how what he read applied to him. When I learned that he had written in the margins of the books, borrowed from the library, we had an issue to address. Phillip's pattern had been to appropriate whatever he wanted and use it as he pleased. Innumerable times, he had stolen or misused property that did not belong to him.

At first, when Phillip made notes about his thoughts, he expected praise for self-restraint: holding himself back from gambling at cards with inmates, not challenging a sheriff's deputy, or not lashing out in a letter to his sister. He behaved as though he ought to receive an award for starting to behave like a civilized human being. I pointed out that people usually do not receive awards for fulfilling obligations. I also pointed out that changing his behavior in one situation did not signify that he had established a new pattern.

Instead of bragging about his achievements, Phillip began to seek feedback from me that would help him improve. Rather than experience a putdown when criticized, he welcomed criticism in order to do better. He became cognizant of thoughts that, to someone else, might seem unimportant, but they contained the seeds of lifelong thinking errors.

I saw the nurse in the hall and thought about running (horseplay) across the unit to be first in line so I would not have to wait in line. Then I thought of the confusion it could bring, possible injury and possible write-up for horseplay. That would put my job in danger and I could end up in a different unit when I am doing good. I am doing my best to make decisions that will not negate the good job I am doing.

In the past, Phillip would pursue single-mindedly what he wanted with little regard to the effect on others. In this situation, Phillip became aware of the thought but did not act on it, deciding instead to think through what was happening. He considered possible immediate consequences to himself, loss of his job assignment, and transfer to a less desirable unit. But he also thought about the impact on others, the "confusion" that dashing across the hall might create. I helped educate Phillip so that he understood that a fleeting thought today could eventually lead to trouble.

Phillip provided another example in which, had he not thought before taking action, he likely would have assaulted another inmate.

Tonight I lent my playing cards to a group of guys so they could have a card game. There were 2 jokers mixed in, and they were not needed. After the cards were dealt, they found the jokers. Someone else said I was stupid for having them in the deck. Little did he know I play a card game where jokers are needed. He picked them up and ripped them in half. I got up and walked over in disbelief. When I realized he had done it I wanted to raise my voice, push him and show my anger and frustration. I gathered myself quickly, walked away, evaluated the situation, walked back and spoke to him. He is not the brightest person. I explained why I was upset. He understood, apologized and said he would buy me a new deck.

The obvious change here was that Phillip chose to restrain himself rather than respond instantly with anger. He took the additional step of explaining calmly to the inmate why he felt as he did. By problem-solving rather than retaliating, Phillip brought about a positive outcome

Eventually, a judge decided to give Phillip another chance and released him on probation. Phillip would continue to meet with me on a regular basis and, periodically, I would write progress reports to the judge. (Phillip had confidentiality with respect to the details of our work together. The reports were to be general in scope, and Phillip would be able to read all of them.) If he failed to cooperate, I would inform his probation officer. If his probation were revoked, Phillip would then have to serve backup time for his earlier offenses as well as additional time for a new probation violation. When I appeared in court on Phillip's behalf, I had no way of knowing whether Phillip's motivation to change would continue. Or perhaps the entire enterprise was a sham played out by a man whose overriding objective was to get out of jail. Only time would tell.

As I write this, Phillip has been out of jail for 11 months. Given that Phillip has never lived a responsible life, we have had innumerable issues to address. As he found a place to live and looked for work, the issues were basic. He arrived late for appointments or confused the time. In the past, being prompt meant nothing. Phillip confided that he was spending hours on the Internet conversing with women all over the world. Although not illegal, this activity was occurring when he should have been looking for a full-time job rather than working sporadically at a restaurant. I learned from the probation officer, who made a home visit, that Phillip's living quarters were "a pig sty." He had never lived on his own and taken care of himself. Either he mooched off family members or was a parasite living with a female.

Phillip became more conscientious about our meetings, calling if he was uncertain about the time and arriving early. After being fired from two jobs for lack of attention to the work, he obtained a fast food restaurant job where he has done well. Issues concerning his treatment of women continue to be addressed. Phillip developed a relationship with Irene, who had just left an abusive marriage. Compared to her ex-husband, Philip was Mr. Wonderful to Irene—a caring, dependable gentleman. (She continued to think the same even after he confided that he was a convicted felon and on probation.) Phillip characterized his relationship with Irene as one of "friends with benefits." Irene did the grocery shopping, cleaned his apartment, cooked meals, took care of his laundry, and had sex with him. She was totally devoted, but her devotion was not reciprocated. While Irene was present, Phillip continued browsing the Internet to converse with females, some of the repartee being sexually explicit. Phillip said that Irene did not object, that she wanted him to do whatever made him happy. Several times, Phillip dated other women, supposedly with Irene not objecting. I asked Phillip if he was willing to have Irene come in and speak with me. He agreed to do this.

Irene affirmed everything that Phillip told me. She showed no resentment about how he treated her. It became evident that Irene had taken such a psychological battering from years of an abusive relationship that she would put up with any man who didn't yell or hit her. She was aware of Phillip's Internet activities and did not object. If Phillip was happy, she was happy.

Although Phillip was doing nothing illegal, he continued to demonstrate thinking errors that had resulted in a lifetime of irresponsibility and criminality. He was the "irresistible" one who dominated this relationship even though Irene did not experience him as controlling. Phillip saw himself as a good guy even though he was exploiting this obviously desperate woman. Phillip continued to view himself as though he were the center of the universe around whom Irene was to revolve. Only what he wanted mattered.

Helping an individual like Phillip change his thinking is an enormous enterprise that goes well beyond equipping him with an education, a job, or social skills. Phillip had graduated from college, held a job, and was very smooth socially. Throughout his adult life, Phillip's education, willingness to work, and superficial social skills helped him deceive others and get away with a great deal. Despite an impressive façade, sometimes because of it, a person's lifelong errors in thinking exact a huge toll.

To gain verification of at least some of what I am being told, I require access to someone who knows the offender well. This is not a customary practice by treatment providers. But it is necessary in counseling a person like Phillip who is self-serving and dishonest. In addition to the weekly two-hour meetings with Phillip, I had contact with members of his family, the probation officer, and access to Irene, who remains willing to talk to me at any time. There continues to be no evidence of illegal activity. Phillip is progressing in much of his day-to-day functioning. A great deal of work remains!

There is no quick fix! Old patterns die hard, if they die at all. Phillip appears to be reaching a point where he has too much to lose to return to crime. There is external leverage: if he violates probation, he will go to the penitentiary. Were that to happen, members of his family would be so devastated that they likely would have little contact with him. Internal motivation has developed since I started working with Phillip when he was in jail. That he has reported, apparently accurately, about his involvement with Irene has provided some indicator of changes. First and foremost, he has been truthful. He could have concealed the entire relationship from me. Second, he has asked for my analysis of the situation. Third, he made Irene available so I could interview her alone. Fourth, he has not been secretive with others. He introduced her to his family, and she introduced him to hers. Recently, Phillip appears to have pangs of conscience. He brought up his past pattern of using a female, then dumping her. He said he worries about hurting Irene.

For three months, we discussed what I referred to as his "abuse" of Irene. As Phillip's family and a longtime female friend got to know Irene and became quite fond of her, they warned Phillip that he better treat her well, or he would surely lose her. Phillip told me repeatedly that he realized he was extremely fortunate to have Irene in his life. She accepted him for who he was, with all his shortcomings. Finally, Phillip informed me he was off the Internet—no more flirting with women! Discussion continues not only about Irene but also about his constant desire to conquer women so that they will love and adore him.

During my career, I have worked with many other offenders in the enterprise of helping them change lifelong thinking errors. I help them become aware of what the errors are, to reject them when they occur (i.e., not act on them), to examine the consequences of the thought patterns, and ultimately, to consider what kind of person they want to be. Only three options exist. The first is to continue to live as they have, which invariably results in their harming others and losing their freedom. The second is to change to living responsibly, a way of life they have envied but with which they have had little experience. The third is not to live at all, to commit suicide, which has occurred fleetingly to some. The men and women whom I have written about in this book have mistakenly believed there is another option, to play both sides of the street. This entails maintaining an appearance of living responsibly while getting away with things on the side. In this, they have succeeded, but only to a point. Eventually, they harm others and dig new holes for themselves.

Change is possible. As he reflected on his past, one man commented, "Some of the things I used to do would make me sick. If I met myself as I was 10 years ago, I wouldn't want anything to do with myself." By becoming aware of thinking errors and understanding their destructive impact, then putting into practice corrective patterns, an offender can become a responsible human being. Instead of being the irresistible, unique, self-centered, controlling person he has always been, he can contribute to others rather than exploit and destroy them. In doing so, he has taken important steps toward transforming his character!

Epilogue

I have taken you with me through the process that I engage in while trying to fathom what appears unexplainable. Without exception, I have found that when a person commits a crime that seems out of character, there is more to the story. In fact, it is not possible to do something out of character. Considering a crime to be "out of character" signifies that we lack information about the personality of the individual.

A crime is the result of thought patterns embedded in the personality of the defendant. A responsible, considerate, compassionate human being does not stalk a teenage girl and commit a brutal rape. A responsible housewife and mother does not address difficulties in her marriage by shooting her husband. A conscientious, dutiful social worker does not enhance her financial position by selling drugs. To understand the dark deeds of intelligent, capable, and often greatly admired people, it is essential to understand how their minds work as they live day to day. All that others know is what they see. People like Stuart, Anna, and Mary successfully erect a façade of respectability. Controlling others is crucial to their self-esteem. However, they maneuver in such a deft manner and they make such a favorable impression that people make generous allowances for their eccentricities. These individuals do not come to the attention of law enforcement authorities. Few consult mental health professionals and, if they do, the contact is brief and superficial. When they get themselves into difficulty, they do their utmost to convert others to their point of view and absolve themselves of culpability.

No one could have predicted the crimes that these individuals committed. They didn't signal their intentions. Friends and relatives knew Wally was upset with Diane, that he was determined to gain custody of his son Kenny. No one, certainly not Diane, had the slightest idea that Wally repeatedly fantasized about killing her. Even the people who thought they knew these perpetrators intimately did not have any idea of what they were capable of doing. Stuart's father saw that he was shy and reclusive. How could he have known that, since childhood, his son had composed pornographic stories that were increasingly violent in nature? Nothing about Mark suggested that he was spending hours hunting for places to expose himself. He always offered a plausible explanation for his absences from home or work. Who could possibly have known that during leisure time on business trips, he'd be casing out sites for his exhibitionism?

In committing the crimes that appeared out of character, these offenders were in fact being true to their own character. Larry feuded with his mother for years and reached a point where he no longer would tolerate her interfering with his plans. He did not premeditate the time, place, and date, or the manner by which he would kill her. Her objection to his California trip turned out to be the one thing too much. Tired of being reined in, Larry freed himself from her restraints forever.

As I said at the outset, we all make thinking errors from time to time. Who among us has not been self-centered? Who has not been overly sensitive to criticism? Who has not harbored unrealistic expectations? Secret controllers are extreme in these and other thinking errors. Their fundamental premise is that life should revolve around them. They arrogantly believe that others must fulfill their expectations. They hold such an inflated, albeit insecure, opinion of themselves that they perceive even a minor criticism, disappointment, or frustration as a threat to their entire self-worth. These individuals do their utmost to control others, but often such control eludes them. Consequently, they are perpetually dissatisfied and simmer with anger at a world that does not accord them what they believe they deserve. Their behavior is an expression of longstanding, but invisible, errors in thinking. Once that thinking is revealed, it becomes evident that their crimes are very much "in character."

Further Reading

American Psychological Association. "Hate Crimes Today: An Age-Old Foe In Modern Dress," Washington, D.C., 1998.

Botkin, Jeffrey R., William M. McMahon & Leslie Pickering Francis (Eds.) *Genetics and Criminality*. Washington, D.C.: American Psychological Association, 1999.

Carey, William. *Understanding Your Child's Temperament*. New York: Macmillan, 1997.

Cohen, David. *Stranger in the Nest*. New York: John Wiley & Sons, 1999.

Douglas, John. *Mind Hunter*. New York: Scribner, 1995.

Furby, Lita, Mark R. Weinrott, & Lyn Blackshaw. "Sex Offender Recidivism: A Review," *Psychological Bulletin*, Vol. 105, No. 1, 1989, pp. 3-30.

Gibbs, Nancy and Timothy Roche. "The Columbine Tapes," *Time*, December 20, 1999, pp. 40-50.

Kendler, Kenneth S. "Parenting: A Genetic-Epidemiologic Perspective," *American Journal of Psychiatry*, 153:1, January 1996, 11-20.

Leap. Terry L. *Dishonest Dollars*. Ithaca: Cornell University Press, 2007.

McPherson, Myra. "The Roots of Evil," *Vanity Fair*, May, 1989, pp. 140ff.

Peleggi, Nicholas. *Wiseguy: Life in a Mafia Family*. New York: Simon & Schuster, 1985.

Satel, Sally and Frederick K. Goodwin. *Is Drug Addiction A Brain Disease?* Washington, D.C. Ethics and Public Policy Center, 1998.

Vise, David. *The Bureau and the Mole*. New York: Atlantic Monthly Press, 2002.

Weinreich, Gil. "Leeson's Lessons," *Research*, January, 2005, pp. 34-40.

White House Conference for a Drug-Free America, *Final Report*, June, 1988.

Index

About the Author

STANTON E. SAMENOW is a forensic psychologist based in Alexandria, Virginia and the author of *Inside the Criminal Mind, Straight Talk about Criminals,* and *Before It's Too Late: Why Some Kids Get into Trouble and What Parents Can Do About It.* He also acted as senior author on a three volume set coauthored with Samuel Yochelson, comprising *The Criminal Personality: A Profile for Change, The Criminal Personality: The Change Process,* and *The Criminal Personality: The Drug User.*